Love in the Mix:
A Cookbook for Romance Readers
To Benefit ProLiteracy

**With contributions from authors of all
genres of romance because love is delicious**

Collected by
Leslie Hachtel & Nikki Brock

With munificent help from Jessa Slade, Judi Fennell,
And with the invaluable support of
Lara Pimentel and Amanda Wilson from ProLiteracy

Acknowledgments

There are not enough words to thank the generous, talented and fabulous authors who took their time and a part of their personal histories and shared them with us so others could have the gift of reading.

Testimonials

Adult literacy can change everything. From health and employment to gender equality and poverty, every social issue is impacted by low literacy. When a person can learn how to read, do basic math, or use a computer, they can lift themselves out of poverty, improve their health, obtain and sustain employment, and ultimately change their lives.

ProLiteracy has received some amazing testimonials from our recipients. Thanks to generous supporters like you, we can continue to provide learning materials and resources for adult literacy programs, tutors, and learners for many years to come.

***

The Collierville Literacy Council recently transitioned to mobile learning.

"We need the Mobile Learning Fund to get [digital] materials to our students. In a recession, our adult learners often suffer the most with unemployment, hunger, evictions, and mental health issues, so helping them quickly with quality material is paramount. We cannot offer digital learning in our program without the Mobile Learning Fund grant resources."

***

Literacy New Jersey now offers student online and phone instruction. They are expanding their digital services to assist students unable to attend in-person, critical for learners who have to balance jobs, families, and other responsibilities.

Our students face a technological divide with unreliable Wi-Fi, no access to computers, and a lack of digital knowledge in something as routine as writing an email.

Our low income, low-literate students are among the most vulnerable and more than ever, our learners need adult literacy instruction as they navigate social systems, and they cannot count on government and other traditional funding sources.

***

"I struggled to obtain my high school equivalency. I lost all motivation to continue and my math teacher grew frustrated when I couldn't grasp the material as quickly as others. I had given up hope of achieving my academic and career goals," said literacy learner Londela.

"Starting at a new adult learning center renewed my self-confidence. The director, staff, and teachers encouraged me, even when I didn't work to my potential. They offered me access to a mobile learning course to help me learn at my own pace. This digital program really helps people, who, like me, are struggling with basic skills because of learning disabilities.

"I couldn't have elevated to the next level without it. Now, I am closer to completing my education and pursing my career as a nursing assistant or a phlebotomist."

Dedication

To the readers, of course.
And to those who are hungry to learn.

Table of Contents

Chapter One Breakfast 1
   Gram's Sour Cream Coffee Cake 3
   Potato Crust Quiche 5
   Wiffle Waffles 8
   Make-Ahead French Toast 9
   Eggvocado Toast 11
   High Protein Breakfasts 13
   Woke Quiche Lorraine 15
   Bangin' Blueberry Muffins 17
   Sunday Morning Cinnamon Pancakes & Whipped Cream 19
Chapter Two Salads 21
   Chilled Tuna Pasta Salad 23
   Spaghetti Salad 25
   Granny's Coke Salad 27
   Heavenly Hash 28
   Dill Pasta Salad 29
   Ella's Smoked Mozzarella and Tomato Salad 31
   Salmon Pasta Salad 33
   Spinach Salad 35
   Spring Salad 36
Chapter Three Appetizers 39
   Adobo Salsa 41
   Tastes-Like-Pizza Dip 42
   Crockpot Hot Artichoke Dip 43
   Spring Cheese 45
   Grilled Jumbo Shrimp 46
   Nisha's Punjabi Samosas 47
   Artichoke Parmesan Dip 49
   Boyos 50
   Borekas 52
Chapter Four Main Dishes 55
   MOM'S ITALIAN STYLE MEAT SAUCE 57

Maryland Crab Cakes 59
Spinach Fritada (Vegetarian) 61
Bleu Cheese Pasta 63
ENCHILADA CASSEROLE... 65
SMOTHERED CHICKEN 67
Bulgogi (Korean grilled beef).. 69
Salmon Bake 71
Baked Ziti... 72
One Pan Salmon and Brussels Sprouts 73
Stuffed Poblanos.. 75
Khichuri... 77
West Texas-Style Cumin-Pepper Steak Tacos............... 79
Pork Carnitas 81
Fish and Potato Pie.. 83
Succulent King Crab Legs.. 85
Baked Catfish 87
Chicken Divan... 88
Mom's Crock Pot Stew.. 89
Beef Burgundy 91
Homemade Tomato Sauce... made with a Food Mill.................. 92
Chorizo Zucchini Tacos for Two...................................... 95
The Easiest Chicken You'll Ever Make............................ 97
Spicy Sausage Pasta 99
Wings Two Ways 101
Seasoned Chicken Wings (dry)...................................... 103
Peanut Butter Chicken Stew 105
Shrimp-Pistachio Pasta.. 106
Dave's Grilled Chicken.. 107
Andie's Spaghetti Sauce with Fresh Pasta..................... 109
Ground Beef Stroganoff 113
Grilled Chicken Skewers 115
Salmon Patties... 117
Go Big or Go Home Lasagna 119
CHEESY CHICKEN 121
Baked Spaghetti... 122
Picnic-Ready Salmon Sandwiches.................................. 123
Parmesan Chicken... 125
Simple Meatloaf 126
Chapter Five Side Dishes 127
Family-Hour Spinach Nuggets 129
Tropical Sweet Potatoes 131
Beans for a Crowd 132

Ella's Stove Top Potatoes 133
Mouth-watering Macaroni and Cheese..................................... 135
Pecan-Raising Turkey Stuffing 137
Sweet & Crunchy Brussels Sprouts... 139
English Roast Potatoes 141
Yorkshire Pudding... 142
Herbed Carrots and Zucchini 143
Cowboy Beans... 144
Thanksgiving Sauerkraut with Pork, Apples, and Onions 145
Oyster Crackers in Savory Herbs 147
Macaroni and Cheese 149
Potato Salad 150
Grandma Willie's Cornbread Dressing 151
Cornbread dressing... 154
Pasta Salad... 155
Judie's Sweet Noodle Kugel.. 157
Marillen or Zwetschgen Knödel (apricot or plum dumplings) 159
Chapter Six Soups... 161
One Pan Chicken and Dumplings Soup 163
Trophy Chili... 165
Sausage Soup 167
Chicken Potato Soup 169
Hubby's Gumbo 171
Kimberly Kincaid's Souper Easy Pumpkin Apple Soup............ 173
Texas Chili- Absolutely No Beans Allowed............................... 175
Bacon and Lentil Soup 177
Chapter Seven Quick Breads 179
Great-Grandma's Drop Biscuits.. 181
Southern Buttermilk Cornbread 183
Almond Loaf.. 184
ROYAL BANANA NUT BREAD.. 185
Irish Brown Bread 187
Massa 189
Lemon Bread 191
Sweet Potato Cornbread... 193
Too good for the bake sale Banana Bread................................ 195
Chapter Eight Cookies.. 197
Kristan's World Famous Chocolate Chip Cookies 199
White Chocolate Fantasy Clusters 200
Grandma Cameron's Scottish Shortbread Cookies 201
LAVENDER SUGAR COOKIES 203
Monster Cookies 205

Pumpkin Walnut Spice Biscotti.. 207
Cadbury Cookies 209
Aunt Dixie's Divinity 211
White Chocolate Raspberry Thumbprints............................... 213
Salted Caramel Shortbread Cookies 215
Triple Ginger Cream Cookies 217
Rum Balls 219
Leslie's Lemon Bars.. 221
Fresh Fruit Cookie Bars 223
Mom's Winter Solstice Cookies 225
Easy-Peasy Buckeyes 227
Rum Balls 229
Almond Biscotti (Tuscan Dipping Cookies)............................. 231
Anzac Slice 233
Chapter Nine Desserts 235
Mud... 237
Trifle.. 239
Cream Puffs.. 241
Nan's Pineapple Soufflé 242
Judi's Apple Pie 243
Mevlyn's Pound Cake 245
White Christmas.. 246
Grandma Loveland's Graham Cracker Pie.............................. 247
Cream Cheese Pound Cake 249
Maine Blackberry Cobbler... 251
Cottage Cheese Pie.. 253
Mocha Oatmeal Cake 255
Chocolate Town Special Cake 257
Creamy Chocolate Under-Frosting... 258
Chocolate Zucchini Cake 259
Vanilla Sugar 261
Better Than Birthday Cake– AKA Better Than Sex Cake 262
Perfect Chocolate Cake 263
Harvest Pie 265
Brownies... 267
Berries with Cream 268
Nisha's Slow Cooker Kheer 269
Pumpkin Roll... 271
Pistachio Cake 273
Pa's Kuchen.. 275
Fabulous Fudge 277
The Best Chocolate Cake.. 278

THE MOST AWESOME CHOCOLATE FUDGE CAKE EVER .. 279
THE MOST AWESOME FUDGE CHOCOLATE ICING 281
Strawberry Pie 282
The Cake of a Thousand Faces 283
Darlene's Lazy Daisy Cake 285
Butter Tarts 287
Polish Apple Cake 289
Polish Plum Cake 290
Bread Pudding 291
Chapter Ten Beverages 293
Margarita – (2 people) or 1 writer who has had a really bad day. . 295
Bloody Mary – (1 person) 296
Hot Spice Wine (for a crowd) 297
Summer Evening White Sangria 298
Chapter Eleven Extra Goodies 301
Steak Marinade 303
Riley's BBQ Sauce 304
'GOING GREENS' SMOOTHIE 306
Quarantine Balls (a/k/a Healthy Granola Treats) 307
Aunt Lee's Hot Fudge 308
Peanut Butter Dog Pill Balls 309
Liver Cookies for Dogs 311
Index 312

Chapter One
Breakfast

Gram's Sour Cream Coffee Cake
Kristan Higgins

At our state fair, there's a baking contest. One of the categories is "Grandma's Best"… basically, a recipe you inherited. I won the blue ribbon the year I entered this, and, years later, so did my daughter when she was only 8 years old! We make it every Christmas Eve so we can enjoy it on Christmas morning, but it's great any time of year.

1. Preheat oven to 350; grease and flour a Bundt cake pan.
2. Sift together 2 cups of all-purpose or gluten-free flour; 1 tablespoon of baking powder; ½ teaspoon salt. Set aside.
3. In mixer, beat together 2 sticks of softened butter and 2 cups of sugar. Add 2 beaten eggs, 1 tablespoon of vanilla extract and 1 cup of sour cream. Beat well. Fold in the dry ingredients by hand and mix well.
4. In separate bowl, combine ¾ cup of sugar and 1 tablespoon of cinnamon. You can add a cup of nuts (pecans, almonds or walnuts) if you like. I think they're better if you toast them first.
5. Put in Bundt pan in the following order:
6. Just enough batter to cover the bottom of the pan.
7. One third of the cinnamon mixture.
8. Two-thirds of the batter.
9. Two-thirds of the cinnamon mixture
10. The remainder of the batter.
11. Bake for 60 minutes.
12. Let sit for 10 minutes, then loosen with a butter knife, lifting the cake up to get air underneath. Invert, and voila!
13. Serve warm with a nice cuppa joe or glass of milk.

***

Kristan Higgins is the New York Times, USA TODAY, Wall Street Journal and Publishers Weekly bestselling author of 19 novels, which have been translated into more than two dozen languages and sold millions of copies worldwide. Her books have received dozens of awards and accolades, including starred reviews from Kirkus, The New York Journal of Books, Publishers Weekly, Library Journal, People and Booklist. If you want to keep up with Kristan's new releases and get a free short story, sign up for her mailing list at www.kristanhiggins.com.

Her books regularly appear on the lists for best novels of the year. Kristan is also a cohost of the Crappy Friends podcast, which discusses the often complex dynamics of female friendships, with her friend and fellow writer, Joss Dey.

The proud descendant of a butcher and a laundress, Kristan lives in Connecticut with her heroic firefighter husband. They own several badly behaved pets and are often visited by their entertaining and long-lashed children.

Potato Crust Quiche
Cathy McDavid

I remember the first time my husband found me standing at the sink eating straight out of a plastic storage container. He asked, "What are you doing?" The question was a rhetorical one, of course. He could clearly see I was standing at the sink and eating. Hmm. What he really meant was, "Why aren't you sitting at the table?" My answer, "I don't want to dirty any dishes," earned me a baffled look.

What? You have to ask the reason I don't transfer my food onto a plate or into a bowl? I get it, dirtying one dish and a couple of utensils doesn't sound like a lot. It's a habit, I suppose, one formed from spending two decades raising kids and caring for a family. All that in addition to working full time and attempting to launch a writing career. Believe me, I hoarded my free minutes like a miser and reduced every chore to the least amount of time possible.

As a result, I learned to eat on the run. As a result of that, I developed a list of favorite foods to devour at the sink with either my fingers, a spoon out of the bowl, or a fork straight from the pan. And if you're wondering, yes, I still do this despite my kids no longer living at home. My husband still hasn't stopped asking why while giving me baffled looks.

Laugh if you will, I just picked up three extra minutes at lunch earlier today.

Fixing meals for a family with very different tastes wasn't easy. From an early age, like, a really early age, my daughter decided she didn't like meat. To this day, she only eats a nibble of fish now and then and maybe a couple bites of turkey at Thanksgiving. That's it. This made meal prepar-ation a real challenge for a lot of years.

One thing she and the whole family always loved was eggs and dairy, especially cheese. Early on, I figured out quiche made a quick, easy meal that earned me no com-plaints. I often prepared two, one with bacon or ham or sausage or even chorizo and the other with no meat. I found this potato crust version years ago and have to say, it's spud-tastic! And nothing like eating a warmed leftover wedge of quiche with my fingers at the sink–right before I rush out the door.

Ingredients:

1 (16 oz) package of frozen shredded hash brown potatoes fully thawed.

5 large eggs (or 6 small ones)

¼ cup melted butter

1 to 1¼ cups shredded Swiss cheese (or cheese of your choice, I also like cheddar and Monterey Jack).

1 cup finely chopped vegetables of choice. Get creative here.

¼ cup milk

1 cup cubed or crumbled breakfast meat of choice.

Your preferred seasonings.

Optional meatless version: use 2 cups finely chopped vegetables rather than 1 cup.

Preheat oven to 375 degrees. Lightly grease a 9-inch pie pan. Press fully thawed shredded potatoes into the pie pan, packing firmly. Brush with melted butter and bake 10 to 15 minutes until golden brown.

In a large bowl, mix together the beaten eggs, milk, cheese, vegetables and optional breakfast meat. Add your seasonings. Pour the mixture evenly over the finished crust. Bake about 20 minutes until center of the quiche is fully set, the top is a lovely brown, and a knife inserted into the center comes out clean.

Perfect for eating with your fingers
Don't forget to add a side: crusty bread and/or fruit salad go well. If you're me, maybe a mimosa!

***

In the third grade, NY Times and USA Today bestselling author **Cathy McDavid** made it her goal to read every Walter Farley book ever written. Who knew such an illustrious ambition would eventually lead to a lifelong love of all things western and a career writing contemporary romances for Harlequin? With over 1.3 million books sold, Cathy is a member of the prestigious Romance Writers of America's Honor Roll. An "almost" Arizona native and mom to grownup twins, she lives with her own real-life sweetheart and spends her days penning stories about good looking cowboys riding the range, busting a bronc, and sweeping gals off their feet. It a tough job, but she's willing to make the sacrifice.

Wiffle Waffles
Deb Kastner

Wiffle Waffles is a favorite breakfast treat that has come down through three generations now. I ate them as a child, made them for my children and now my grand-children. It's easy to make and yummy to eat as a special occasion or just a weekend brunch with family.

1. Heat oven to 450 degrees
2. Melt 1/2 stick butter in 9" X 12" glass baking dish
3. Mix: 1/2 cup flour, 1/2 cup milk and 2 eggs
4. Pour into baking dish and bake 12-15 minutes.
5. Sprinkle with powdered sugar if desired.

***

Publishers Weekly Bestselling, award-winning author of over 50 novels and over 2 million books in print, **Deb Kastner** enjoys writing contemporary romances, romantic comedies and cowboy romances set in small towns.

Deb lives in beautiful Colorado with her husband, two adorable dogs and two mischievous cats. For her midlife crisis she recently (finally!) adopted a horse, a three-year-old Arabian gelding named Moscato.

She is blessed with three adult daughters and two grandchildren. Her favorite hobby is spoiling her grandchildren, but she also enjoys reading, binge-watching television, listening to music (The Texas Tenors are her fav), singing in the church choir and exploring the Rocky Mountains on horseback.

Make-Ahead French Toast
RaeAnne Thayne

I make this every Christmas morning, along with a Farmer's Breakfast casserole. Both are easy to throw together Christmas Eve. I toss them in the oven while we open presents and the house is soon filled with delicious smells, with very little work on my part!

Ingredients
    5 eggs, lightly beaten
    1 ½ cups milk
    1 cup half-and-half cream
    1 t vanilla extract
    ½ loaf French bread, cut diagonally in 1 inch slices (I use Texas toast)
    ½ cup butter, melted
    1 cup light brown sugar
    2 T maple syrup
    1 cup chopped pecans

Directions
1. In a large bowl, whisk together eggs, milk, cream and vanilla.
2. Dip bread slices into egg mixture and place in a lightly greased 9x13 inch baking pan.
3. Refrigerate overnight.
4. The next morning, preheat oven to 350 degrees F.
5. In a small bowl, combine butter, sugar, maple syrup and pecans.
6. Spoon mixture over bread.
7. Bake in preheated oven until golden, about 40 minutes.
8. Let stand 5 minutes before serving.

***

New York Times, USA Today and #1 Publishers Weekly bestselling author **RaeAnne Thayne** finds inspiration in the beautiful northern Utah mountains where she lives with her family. Her stories have been described as "poignant and sweet," with "beautiful, honest storytelling that goes straight to the heart."

Eggvocado Toast
Aliza Mann

Makes 2 servings

I have never loved avocado on its own, despite the health benefits. But this little twist to avocado toast makes it one of my favorite breakfast meals.

Ingredients:
  2 large eggs
  I large avocado
  1 small hot house tomato
  ½ small red onion (or half of a medium)
  ½ teaspoon of salt
  ½ teaspoon of black pepper
  ½ teaspoon of garlic salt
  1 lime (or two teaspoons of lime juice)

Directions:
1. In a small sauce pan, boil eggs for 6 – 10 minutes to hard boiled state.
2. In a medium sized bowl, core and dice avocado
3. Mince tomatoes. red onion, and add salt, black pepper, and garlic salt (season to taste) and lightly mix all ingredients with avocado.
4. Dice slightly cooled eggs and fold into avocado mixture.
5. Drizzle lime juice and stir until mixed.
6. Serve over toasted brioche bun or whole grain wheat toast cut into halves.

Recipe Notes:
- The lime juice will prevent avocado from turning brown, but dish is best if eaten within 2 days.
- Best with ripened avocado.

***

Ever since she was a small child, **Aliza Mann** loved to tell stories. It started in the backyard of her family's home where she shared them with the neighborhood kids. Through the years she read anything she could get her hands on. In high school she found her love for romance. From the moment she opened the cover of a romantic historical page-turner, she found herself hooked.

Actively employed, she balances her love of writing a great story between two pseudo-adult children, a fabulous son-in-law, and the man of her dreams. A true book nerd, she is almost always reading and writing the world in a way that shows its true beauty, served with a heaping side of *happily ever after.*

High Protein Breakfasts
Gemma Brocato

I try to focus on adding protein to my diet, because everyone says carbs are bad (explain that to my regular servings of chips and popcorn). But I found it was easy to get stuck in an eggs and bacon rut to satisfy a low carb, high protein breakfast. I'm always on the lookout for ways to get protein without cracking an egg. Here are two options I really like.

High Protein Greek Yogurt Breakfast
½ cup of nonfat Greek yogurt
¼ tsp of sugar free Jell-O mix or one squirt of Mio drink mix – your choice of flavor
One serving of fruit, such as apple or peach
Spices to flavor, like cinnamon or nutmeg
Optional: a small amount (1-2 tsp) of granola or nuts

Directions
1. Mix the Jell-O powder or Mio with Greek yogurt until blended.
2. Cut in the fruit and add whatever spices you choose. I use apples and cinnamon with black cherry or cranberry raspberry Jell-O, but when peaches are in season, I reach for peach Jell-O, cinnamon, and cloves (tastes a little like the pickled peaches my mom used to make). The fun part of this recipe is how creative you get to be.
3. Top with granola or nuts if you want a little more crunch.

Bonus! High Protein Pancakes

I love these pancakes and prefer to make mine with ricotta cheese, because I think they turn out creamier than when I use cottage cheese. This recipe makes 8 pancakes but can be cut down accordingly.
Ingredients

8 oz of low-fat ricotta or cottage cheese

1 /4 cup egg substitute (Like Egg Beaters – you only want to use the whites)

2 scoops of vanilla protein powder (or chocolate is always good too)

Directions

1. Mix everything together.
2. Heat skillet over medium high heat, and coat with a cooking spray.
3. Pour a dollop of the mixture in the pan, and cook until brown on one side. Flip and continue cooking until done.

I top these pancakes with peanut butter or almond butter. You can serve it with a side of fresh fruit or a fruit smoothie, but be careful, because that will add in carbs.

***

Gemma Brocato's favorite desk accessories for many years were a circular wooden token, better known as a 'round tuit,' and a fortune from a fortune cookie that said she was a lover of words; someday she'd write a book. She always knew that eventually she'd get around to writing the novel trapped in her mind. It took a transfer to the United Kingdom, the lovely English springtime, and a huge dose of homesickness to write her first novel. Once it was completed and sent off with a kiss even the rejections, addressed to 'Dear Author', were gratifying.

After returning to America, she spent a number of years as a copywriter, dedicating her skills to making insurance and the agents who sell them sound sexy. Eventually, her full-time job as a writer interfered with her desire to be a writer full-time and she left the world of financial products behind to pursue an avocation as a romance author.

Her gamble paid off when she was a 2012 Finalist in the prestigious Golden Pen contest for Romantic Suspense and she received contracts for her first and second book.

Woke Quiche Lorraine
Heather Heyford

I was shocked and dismayed to read in a well-respected journal that quiche Lorraine (named for the region in France) is nowadays considered a throwback to the days of shoulder pads and big hair.

One of the nice things about having lived through the Shoulder-Pads-and-Big-Hair-Era is no longer giving a flying fig what foods happen to be in style (likewise, bicycle shorts and coloring my hair the shade of blue once seen only at carnival, cotton candy booths).

Quiche has been, and, IMHO, always will be a classic, go-to dish for family brunches and to impress overnight guests–and for many, excellent reasons. Quiche is quick, easy, nutritious and inexpensive to make. It can be varied in ways limited only by the type of produce and cheese you happen to have on hand. It will make your kitchen smell like a French farmhouse. When pulled from the oven–preferably while wearing cute, red and white gingham oven mitts–its puffy, golden brown goodness elicits mouth-watering gasps of anticipation.

Having said all that, recent circumstances have forced me to make a concession to tradition: our family's quiche must now be crust-free. Food sensitivities–real or imagined–are in vogue, thanks in large part to a few, svelte actresses-turned-lifestyle gurus. But where there's a legitimate diagnosis of celiac disease, avoiding gluten isn't just a fad. It's a necessity.

Fortunately, the crust isn't the most flavorful part. We barely notice it's gone. Our waistlines don't miss the extra saturated fat and calories. And I have to admit, I feel a tiny bit smug knowing that, even if purely by happenstance, our quiche has been brought into the twenty-first century.

Ingredients

> 12 slices crisply cooked bacon, crumbled. Alternative: cubed, cooked ham. For vegetarian quiche, do not add meat.
>
> 3 cups shredded Swiss cheese (about 8 oz.) Alternatives: cheddar, gruyere
>
> ⅓ onion, minced
>
> 8 eggs, lightly beaten
>
> 1 c. half and half
>
> salt and pepper to taste
>
> scant 1/8 tsp. cayenne pepper
>
> Optional add ins: chopped, fresh asparagus, spinach, or mush-rooms; or frozen spinach, thawed and drained with the liquid pressed out.

(If you end up with too much filling, cook the excess in a greased pan on the stove, omelet-style.)

Directions

1. Preheat oven to 425.
2. Using butter or cooking spray, grease a glass or ceramic pie pan (not deep dish). Set it on a baking sheet to catch spills.
3. Sprinkle bacon, cheese and onion evenly in pie pan. In a large bowl, beat together remaining ingredients except cayenne, and pour into pie pan. Sprinkle cayenne on top. Cook uncovered about 40 minutes.
4. Reduce oven temperature to 300. Continue to cook about 30 minutes or more, until a knife inserted comes out clean. Let sit about 10 minutes before serving.

Bon appetit!

***

Heather Heyford writes contemporary romance novels set in the wine country, where she visits frequently to drink pinot noir–er, research books.

Heather sold her first romance series in 2014 to Kensington Publishing's then-new digital imprint, Lyrical Press. After gaining a following in digital, her mass market paperback series launched in 2018 with The Sweet Spot, a contemporary love story set in Oregon's Willamette Valley.

Bangin' Blueberry Muffins
Casey Hagen

This recipe is legendary in my family...and even more so since I doubled the blueberries to two cups! The best part...people who claim to hate oatmeal don't even realize it has any in it. Just ask my brother. He was horrified to find out he'd been betrayed by his family and the muffins for more than three decades!

Ingredients
   ½ cup orange juice
   ½ cup quick oats
   ½ cup vegetable oil (if you want to make these lower fat, you
       can substitute apple sauce for the oil)
   ½ cup granulated sugar
   1 egg
   2 cups blueberries
   1½ cups flour
   ¼ tsp. baking soda
   1¼ tsp. baking powder

Directions
1. Blend sugar, oil, and egg.
2. Add the dry ingredients.
3. Then fold in freshly washed blueberries.
4. Spoon into greased or paper lined muffin tins filling each tin 2/3 full.
5. Sprinkle with cinnamon sugar and bake at 400 degrees for 18-20 minutes.

***

USA Today Bestselling author **Casey Hagen** takes her pen and jabs it straight into the heart of her readers. Sometimes penning romantic suspense, sometimes lighter stories, every single one of her books holds a hint of angst and romance that will leave you panting for more.

Born and raised in New England, she's got Ben & Jerry's beating in her heart, and real Vermont maple syrup dripping through her veins.

She's got an insatiable addiction to Fall Out Boy and the new Taylor Swift album, Folklore, because...AMAZEBALLS. Oh, and a new, rather concerning obsession with tattoos and piercings.

If you're searching for her, she's usually found sitting at her command terminal planning to take over the world. When she takes back the pen she's stabbed into her readers' hearts, she creates beautifully brutal romance between fierce women and the men who topple off their alpha thrones for them.

And she thanks every last one of you who picks up one of her stories.

Casey is done talking about herself in the third person now.

Casey out

Sunday Morning Cinnamon Pancakes
& Whipped Cream
Catherine Stuart

This recipe comes from my grandmother, who never cared for syrup on her pancakes. She thought it was too sweet and ruined the flavor. Whipped cream seems almost too rich for breakfast, but it can't be anymore decadent than maple syrup, right? I make this breakfast for special occasions – Father's Day breakfast-in-bed, birthdays, and Sundays just-because. The aroma is amazing, and it will make your kitchen smell like cinnamon and vanilla for hours.

Pancake Batter Ingredients
Dry Ingredients
> 2 cups all-purpose flour
> ¼ cup sugar
> 1 tbsp. + 1 tsp. baking powder
> 1 tsp. salt
> 1 tsp. cinnamon

Wet Ingredients
> 2 cups milk
> ¼ cup unsalted butter, melted (in the microwave)
> 2 eggs
> 1 tsp. vanilla

Whipped Cream Ingredients
> 1 cup heaving whipping cream
> 2 tbsp. powdered sugar
> 1 tsp. cinnamon

Step 1. Prep your ingredients/ tools.
1. Chop up the butter and place into a coffee cup. Cook in the microwave for about 45 seconds, until melted.
2. Put a large mixing bowl in the freezer. You will need an extra-cold bowl for making the whipped cream.

Step 2. Prepare the pancake batter.
1. Mix the dry ingredients together in a bowl.
2. In a separate bowl, mix together all of the wet ingredients except the butter. Pour the melted butter into the milk/egg mixture very slowly, whisking as you go. If you pour the butter into the bowl all at once, it will turn into one giant chunk of butter, floating on top. Either that, or the hot butter will cook the eggs.
3. Slowly pour the wet ingredients into the bowl with the dry ingredients, stirring as you go. Don't overmix, or your pancakes will taste gummy.

Step 3. Cook the pancakes.
1. Heat up a griddle or large fry pan. Personally, I like to cook my pancakes on low. It takes longer, but it means I don't have to throw any out for getting burned. I also prefer smaller pancakes, using about a ¼ cup of batter per pancake. You will know when the pancakes are ready to be flipped because little bubbles will form in the pancake batter.

Step 4. Make the whip cream.
1. Pull your mixing bowl out of the freezer.
2. Place whipping cream, powdered sugar, and cinnamon into the bowl and using a hand mixer, mix until you get stiff peaks. Don't over-mix, or you will churn your cream into butter. You can also use a whisk instead. This works better if you are ambidextrous, and you can trade back and forth between your arms as you tire them out whisking.

Step 5.
1. Top your pancakes with a spoonful of cinnamon whipped cream, and bask in the glory of your creation.

Note:
Recipe makes enough for two adults and two kids, with plenty leftover to freeze. To serve after freezing, microwave for 15 seconds, and then pop in the toaster.

***

Catherine Stuart works as a data geek by day and a novelist by night, spinning tails with quirky heroines and flirty romance. Her first novel was a finalist for the Romance Writers of America's Golden Heart® Award, and she is currently hard at work writing the next three books in the series, following the adventurous of the Beachamp sisters. Catherine lives in coastal Maine with her hot husband, two rambunctious kids, one fluffy dog, and a demonic cat.

Chapter Two
Salads

Chilled Tuna Pasta Salad
Cathy McDavid

Perfect for eating with a fork straight from the bowl

Okay, so a little back story on this family favorite dish. Unlike me, my mom was an excellent cook. She made this tuna and macaroni salad often during the summer when I was growing up, and it was a family favorite. We loved having cold dinners, as she called them, and eating on the back patio. It was, and still is, a real treat.

I do have a confession to make. Despite following Mom's recipe exactly, my dish has never tasted as good as hers. I guess there's something special about your mom's cooking. Even though mine isn't as good, I love the memories the dish evokes every time I make it.

Ingredients:
   1 package shell macaroni (or other pasta of choice but small pasta works best)
   ½ cup frozen green peas, thawed
   2 cans (5 oz each) tuna, drained (I also like the tuna that comes in a pouch)
   1 cup mayonnaise or salad dressing
   2-3 tablespoons bottled Italian dressing to taste
   1 medium stalk celery, chopped (1/2 cup)
   1small onion or bunch of green onions, finely chopped (1/4 cup)
   Your preferred seasonings
   Can also add chopped cucumber, red peppers and/or radish if desired. Also, for a change of pace, substitute two teaspoons lemon juice for the Italian dressing.

Preparation:

1. Cook macaroni as directed on package, adding peas for last 4 to 6 minutes of cooking; drain and rinse with cold water until pasta is room temperature.
2. In large bowl, mix the macaroni, peas, and remaining ingredients. Cover and refrigerate for at least 1 hour to blend flavors - two hours is better. If the salad seems dry after chilling, add a dollop more mayonnaise and Italian dressing to moisten.

This dish pairs extremely well with chilled summer salads, like spinach or cucumber.

Spaghetti Salad
Mindy Neff

I got this recipe from a friend in California forty-five years ago and it's been one of my go-to potluck dishes ever since. Plus, my kids love it, so it makes a wonderful summer salad to go with hamburgers and hotdogs or barbeque chicken and corn on the cob! I love anything I can make the day ahead of company or parties. This makes a huge dish to serve a crowd, and it's super yummy!! Because I have some picky family members who don't like onions, I'll often scoop out a portion and leave out the onions. It's good either way. But if your family likes onions, put them in.

Ingredients
   --2 Lbs. thin spaghetti (cooked)
   --1 large bottle of Wishbone Italian dressing
   --1 red onion (diced)
   --1 or 2 burpless English cucumbers (diced)
   --4 or 5 tomatoes (diced)
   --1 bottle Salad Supreme (I use McCormick)

Mix all ingredients in a large bowl. Best if made the night before and chilled.

***

Mindy Neff is the award-winning author of over thirty novels and novellas. Her contemporary romances touch the heart, tug at the reader's emotions, and always, without fail, have a happy ending. Mindy is the recipient of the National Reader's Choice Award, the Orange Rose Award of Excellence, the Romantic Times Career Achievement award and the Romantic Times Reviewer's Choice Award, as well as W.I.S.H. awards for outstanding heroes, and two prestigious RITA nominations. Originally from Louisiana, Mindy moved to Southern California where she met and married a very romantic guy a little over thirty years ago. They blended their families, his three kids and her two, and have been living happily (if a little insanely) ever after. Now, when she isn't meddling in the lives of her five kids and ten grandchildren, Mindy hides out with a good book, hot sunshine, and a chair at the river's edge at her second home along the Parker Strip in Arizona.

Granny's Coke Salad
Mindy Neff

This was my mom's recipe and it showed up on every holiday table. I love the flavors of cream cheese, nuts and cherries. Yum!

Ingredients
    --Two small boxes black cherry Jello
    --Two 8oz can's coca cola
    --1 Pkg. Cream Cheese
    --1 Cup pecans
    --1 can black bing cherries–pitted
    --1 can pineapple chunks

Directions
1. Mix Jello with the juice from the fruit (cherries and pineapple) and bring to a boil.
2. Remove from heat and add cokes.
3. When it starts to gel, add fruit and nuts.
4. Pinch off pieces of cream cheese and drop evenly over the top.
5. Chill until set.

Heavenly Hash
Teri Wilson

This recipe is a sentimental favorite that my mother used to make during the holidays when I was a little girl. It's sweet and fluffy and always reminds me of my mom and the ballet, because my cousins were principal dancers in the Houston Ballet. Late on Christmas Eve, after the final performance of The Nutcracker, they'd join the family party with all their dancer friends, and I was always so dazzled by them while I enjoyed this favorite special dish.

Ingredients
1 large can crushed pineapple (drained)
1 large package tiny marshmallows
2 half-pint sized cartons of whipping cream
6 bananas, sliced up

Directions
1. Soak pineapples and marshmallows overnight.
2. The next day—whip cream with electric mixer until fluffy.
3. Add remaining ingredients and stir together. (Add coconut, if desired.)

Makes a very large sized bowl.

***

Teri Wilson is a USA TODAY bestselling author of heartwarming, whimsical contemporary romance and Hallmark Channel movies. Lover of crowns, cute dogs and pretty dresses.

Dill Pasta Salad
Gail Chianese

This is a family favorite. Even my pickiest eater loves this salad (and he hates mayonnaise and eggs). About a million years ago (okay, more like 30), when my oldest was just a baby, my mom starting throwing ingredients together for a quick lunch. This is what she came up with. I still remember that first time she was holding my 6-month-old daughter in one arm and the block of cheese with the same hand. As she grabbed for something, my daughter leaned over and tried to eat the cheese. She's been a fan of cheese ever since, and like her brothers, loves this dish. It's great any time of the year or to take to a potluck or picnic.

Ingredients
 1 box of farfalle or small shell pasta
 2 good size chicken breasts, skinless, boneless
 4 oz of sharp cheddar cheese, cubed
 3 large hard-boiled eggs, chopped
 3 large dill pickles, chopped
 ¼ c. of mayonnaise
 Olive oil
 Dill weed
 Garlic
 Salt and Pepper

Directions
1. Boil pasta, drain and let cool.

2. While your pasta is cooking, drizzle a little olive oil in a large skillet. Dice the chicken breast and grill over medium-high heat until done. About ten minutes or so, depending on skillet size. While the chicken is cooking, sprinkle dill weed, garlic, salt, and pepper on the chicken. I never actually measure this part, so I'm going to say about 1 tsp of dill weed and a good shake of the others. If you love garlic, add more.

3. Once the chicken has cooked, let it cool to the touch. Now, mix your pasta, chicken, cheese, eggs, pickles in a large bowl. Mix in the mayonnaise. Again, I don't generally measure this so, I'm guestimating here. You want your pasta moist but not saturated. Sprinkle about 1 tablespoon of dill weed and mix into the pasta.

4. Important: taste test it at this point. Does it need more dill? More garlic? Salt & Pepper? If so, add it.

5. Once you've got the right taste (and you'll know because it'll taste good to you), cover and chill in the refrigerator. It can be made the day before, but the pasta tends to absorb the mayo, so you may need to add a bit more before serving.

Enjoy.

***

Gail Chianese is a multi-published author of contemporary romance, romantic mystery, and women's fiction. Originally from California, (she's lived in eight states and three countries thanks to the US Navy) and now calls Connecticut home with her real-life hero of a husband, her three amazing kids and too many animals to count.

Ella's Smoked Mozzarella and Tomato Salad
Ella Quinn

I've had this recipe for so long I can't even remember when I first started making it. What I can tell you is I've had guys fight to be first in line at cookouts. This recipe serves 4, but it can be easily doubled or tripled for a larger group.

Ingredients
12 ounces smoked Mozzarella (available almost everywhere these days) chopped.
3 pints ripe cherry tomatoes halved
1 cup packed fresh basil leaved shredded

Ella's White Wine Vinaigrette
Equal amounts of white-wine vinegar and good quality olive oil, but in a shaker bottle or bowl. Add about 2 teaspoons French style mustard and two peeled garlic cloves smashed or cut in half. Shake or combine with a whisk until the oil and vinegar are well combined.

Preparation
1. In a bowl combine the mozzarella, tomatoes, and basil.
2. In a small bowl whisk the vinegar and olive oil until it is combined.
3. Mix the dressing with the tomatoes, being careful not to use too much. Keep covered for at least 20 minutes before serving. Do not refrigerate. It will make the tomatoes mealy.

***

USA Today bestselling author **Ella Quinn's** studies and other jobs have always been on the serious side. Reading historical romances, especially

Regencies, were her escape. Eventually her love of historical novels led her to start writing them.

She is married to her wonderful husband of over thirty years. They have a son and two beautiful granddaughters, and a Portuguese Water Dog. After living in the South Pacific, Central America, North Africa, England and Europe, she and her husband decided to make their dreams come true and are now living on a sailboat. After cruising the Caribbean and North America, she completed a transatlantic crossing from St. Martin to Southern Europe. She's currently living in Germany, happily writing while her husband is back at work, recovering from retirement.

Salmon Pasta Salad
Piper G. Huguley

This recipe is an invention of mine whenever I had leftover salmon. Now, I make extra salmon on purpose to make this recipe from scratch because we have come to love it. In any case, you need to use fresh salmon, not canned for this recipe.

Ingredients
½ pound fresh salmon (whatever kind you like)
¼ cup extra virgin olive oil + 1 tablespoon extra virgin olive oil
2 teaspoons dill
1 cup orzo pasta
1 cup chopped cooked broccoli (use fresh) or 1 cup chopped fresh/ frozen spinach
2 tablespoons lemon juice (can be from fresh lemons or RealLemon juice)
½ cup shredded (not grated) parmesan cheese
2 green onions chopped fine (optional)

Directions
1. Drizzle one tablespoon extra-virgin olive oil on the salmon and sprinkle with 2 teaspoons of dill. Broil or bake the salmon. Set aside or refrigerate until ready to make pasta salad.
2. Put the orzo in a pan and fill it with water until there is an inch of water covering the pasta. Boil the orzo for about 12 minutes. Pour off the pasta water and set aside. Do not throw it away and do not rinse the orzo.
3. In the pan where the orzo is, pour on the remaining olive oil, the vegetable that you chose, the lemon juice and stir over a low flame. Stir continuously or the cheese will clump up. If it does, use a little of the pasta water to thin it out.
4. Flake the salmon and add it to the pasta. Stir and serve with a green salad for a main meal or with fish if it's a side.

Serves 6 as a side or 3 for dinner

***

Piper G. Huguley is a two-time Golden Heart ®finalist and author of two historical romance series: "Migrations of the Heart", about the Great Migration and "Home to Milford College." Her contemporary romance debut comes out in 2021 with Hallmark Publishing. She will make her historical fiction debut in March 2022 with William Morrow with a book about Ann Lowe, the Black fashion designer of Jackie Kennedy's wedding dress.

She lives in Atlanta, Georgia with her husband and son.

Spinach Salad
Dee Davis

I had a wonderful spinach salad years ago in a restaurant in Albuquerque with my mother. It had the perfect combination of flavor and texture. I was determined to create my own version, and that recipe evolved into a family favorite.

Ingredients
5 oz pkg baby spinach
8 oz pkg goat cheese (can use crumbled feta as well)
1 small purple onion
1 cup candied pecan pieces
Roasted Red Pepper Dressing

Directions
1. Thinly slice onion and crumble cheese.
2. Mix cheese and onion with spinach.
3. Add candied pecan pieces. Toss.
4. Serve with roasted red pepper dressing. (We use Annie's.)

Candied Pecans

Mix 1/2 cup firmly packed brown sugar, 2 tablespoons orange juice and 1 cup Pecan pieces. Spread pecan mixture on baking sheet covered with parchment paper and bake at 350 for 10-12 minutes. Cool and break apart. Keep in refrigerator if not using immediately.

***

Bestselling author **Dee Davis** is the author of over thirty novels, including award winning time travel romance and romantic suspense. When not frantically trying to meet a deadline, Dee spends her time in her Connecticut farmhouse with her husband and Cardigan Welsh Corgis.

Spring Salad
Sheila Roberts

I'm never going to have my own cooking show, but I do like to experiment in the kitchen. This spring salad is one I concocted when I wanted to do something new with asparagus. I love it because it's so easy to make. I can even get my husband, Mr. Meat is the Only Vegetable I Know, to eat it.

My mother was a stay-at-home mom and a kitchen queen. I can still remember coming home from school to the aroma of chocolate chip cookies baking in the oven. To me, cookies say love. In fact, anything baked says love! I especially like these lavender cookies. I've become a big fan of using lavender in cakes and cookies, and I grow English lavender just so I can have those buds on hand. You can, of course, buy lavender buds online. But, if you've got a flower bed or room on your patio or apartment balcony for a pot, why not grow some yourself? Then you can use it in these lovely cookies, which are perfect for tea parties with girlfriends. By the way, a quick shout out to all those bloggers who work so hard to create recipes we all can enjoy. Several offer basic sugar cookie recipes, all of which contain the same ingredients, but the one I used for my jumping off point I got years ago from Allrecipes.com.

Ingredients:
2 cups asparagus, cut up
½ cup finely chopped orange or red bell pepper
2 green onions, finely chopped
½ cup cut up cherry tomatoes
1 cup grated mozzarella cheese
2 Tbsp olive oil dressing

Directions:
1. Cut asparagus into small, bite-sized pieces – enough to fill two cups – and steam until almost tender. Drain and cool.
2. Cut the cherry tomatoes (I use the yellow ones) in half until you have half a cup's worth and add to the chilled asparagus along with pepper and onion.
3. Mix in cheese and add dressing.
4. Chill well before serving.

Serves 4 generously

***

With nearly thirty books to her name, **Sheila Roberts** is a frequent USA Today and Publishers Weekly bestseller – and a fan favorite. Her Christmas perennial "On Strike for Christmas" was made into a movie for the Lifetime Channel and her novel "The Nine Lives of Christmas" was made into a movie for Hallmark. Her novel "Angel Lane" was listed as one of Amazon's Best Books of the Year. Before settling into her writing career, Sheila owned a singing telegram company and played in band. When she's not traveling, Sheila splits her time between the Pacific Northwest and Southern California.

Chapter Three
Appetizers

Adobo Salsa
K.D. Garcia

My mother-in-law taught me how to cook Mexican food–with lard, full-fat cheese, and rich cream. My family loves it. Below is a recipe that focuses on the flavors the chiles bring to the food, which are much healthier and just as yummy.

Ingredients
 3-4 plum tomatoes roasted with skin off*
 2-4 cloves of garlic
 1 small white onion
 6-8 chipotles in adobo (or fresh jalapenos roasted with skin off*)
 Kosher salt to taste

Place all ingredients in a food processor and puree. Enjoy with tortilla chips, on eggs, or on top of stuffed poblanos.

NOTE: Chipotles have a wonderful smoky flavor. If you prefer a fresher, crisper flavor, swap the chipotles for jalapenos, but make sure you roast the peppers and remove the skin and seeds.

***

A practicing veterinarian, when not at work, **K.D. Garcia** enjoys the chaos her usually wonderful children, mostly well-behaved dogs, and somewhat devious cats bring to life. She's grateful for her typically tolerant husband.

 When she finds time for herself, she spends it reading or writing. She writes contemporary romance, young adult, and middle grade books. Like her life, her stories are infused with animals.

Tastes-Like-Pizza Dip
Sarah Andre

Stand back and wait for the effusive compliments! Maybe bet a few people as they try to guess the ingredients, because this tastes *exactly* like a cheesy pepperoni pizza! The first time I sampled this delicious dip I went from guest to guest tracking down the guest who brought it. (Crazed hostess!) But I found her and got the recipe.

So easy and quick to make that even my 93 year-old dad makes it for his parties!

Ingredients:
8oz softened cream cheese
A 10.5 oz can of Campbell's Cream of Mushroom soup
A 6 oz pkg of Hormel sliced pepperoni, cut into large flakes, reserving
¼ cup.
Bag of Tostito Scoops or your tortilla chip of choice.

Directions
1. Preheat oven to 350°
2. Mix together the cream cheese and mushroom soup until well blended. Stir in the pepperoni bits. Pour into a greased pie dish. Top with the remaining ¼ cup of pepperoni.
3. Bake approximately 30 min- you want the top to be brown and bubbling.
4. Serve with tortilla chips.

***

Sarah Andre is a 2017 RITA® finalist, which is Romance Writers of America highest award of distinction. She lives in serene Southwest FL with her husband and two naughty Pomeranians. When she's not writing, Sarah is either reading novels, exercising to rude alternative rock music or coloring. Yes, you heard right. She's all over hose coloring books for adults.

Crockpot Hot Artichoke Dip
Beth Carter

Who doesn't love spinach artichoke dip? This recipe is delicious and frees up the oven. Be prepared to hear a lot of "oohs and ahhhs."

Ingredients
- 2 14 oz. jars marinated artichoke hearts, drained
- 1 cup mayonnaise
- 1 cup sour cream
- 1 cup water chestnuts, chopped
- 2 cups grated parmesan cheese
- ¼ cup scallions, chopped (may substitute onion salt)

Directions
1. Cut artichoke hearts into half-inch pieces. And mayonnaise, sour cream, water chestnuts, and parmesan cheese. Stir well and place in a slow cooker.
2. Cook on high 1-2 hours or on low 3-4 hours. This is an easy, delicious dip! Serve with crackers, chips, or even cucumber slices.

Serves: 6-8

***

Beth Carter writes humorous, heartwarming women's fiction and romantic comedy including the popular Coconuts series. She also pens children's picture books, wrote *THE QUARANTINE COOKBOOK* for charity during the pandemic, and has recently written a book on writing, publishing, and marketing titled *I WROTE A BOOK*. If the author isn't writing, she's likely sucked into the social media vortex, shopping at T.J. Maxx, or staring at deer in her backyard. Carter splits her time between her home state of Missouri and sunny Florida.

Spring Cheese
Dee Davis

The *heuriger* is an institution in certain parts of Austria. Particularly in the hill country surrounding Vienna. Started in feudal days it was a way to share freshly made wine with neighbors and friends. This is an Americanized version of *fruhlingskase*, a garlicy spread for crackers or bread. Since not all of the Austrian counterparts are available here, I adapted the recipe accordingly upon moving home.

Ingredients
4 oz cream cheese
1 stick butter
1 ½ oz goat cheese
1 ½ tsp dried parsley (can use fresh chopped if available)
3 cloves garlic, minced or pressed

Directions
1. Mix cheeses and butter until creamy (can use a mixer or even a food processor).
2. Add the chopped garlic and parsley.
3. Season with salt. If the cheese is too firm, stir in a Tbs sour cream. Should be spreadable.
4. Serve with fresh dark bread and of course lots of wine!

***

Bestselling author **Dee Davis** is the author of over thirty novels, including award winning time travel romance and romantic suspense. When not frantically trying to meet a deadline, Dee spends her time in her Connecticut farmhouse with her husband and Cardigan Welsh Corgis.

Grilled Jumbo Shrimp
Susan Wisnewski

You want it elegant yet don't have a ton of time to fuss. I've got you covered. This is simple to prepare and big on flavor. And who doesn't love shrimp? Best of all, purchase at your local fishmonger and ask for them to peel and devein leaving tails on and this recipe is a breeze.

Ingredients
¾ lb. Jumbo Shrimp, peeled, deveined, tail intact
¼ cup Extra Virgin Olive Oil
1 TBS Lemon Juice
¼ tsp Salt
Fresh Ground Pepper to taste
½ tsp minced Garlic
1 tsp chopped Fresh Parsley

Directions
1. Mix all of the ingredients together, except the shrimp in a bowl.
2. Add the shrimp and toss lightly.
3. Let marinate refrigerated for about 1 hour turning once or twice.
4. Heat a ridged cast iron pan or heavy-duty frying pan. When pan is hot, place shrimp on the pan. Let cook about 3-4 minutes per side. The shrimp will begin to curl.
5. Serve the shrimp with a crusty baguette, mopping up the juices.

***

Susan Peterson Wisnewski is an indie author from the east coast. She writes thrillers and mystery with a sprinkling of horror.
From a cruncher of numbers to a stringer of words, she decided it was time to follow her dreams and put down on paper all of those stories that floated around in her head.
Surprise and twists keep her readers guessing and she has been accused of writing books that can't be put down. Pushing characters to challenge themselves is her trademark as is a creating strong female characters – no damsels in distress.

Nisha's Punjabi Samosas
Nisha Sharma

I think every book I've ever written so far has referenced samosas. It's a fried pocket with an explosion of flavor inside! What's not to love about it? If you'd love the perfect snack pairing for one of my books, this is definitely the one.

Prep Time: 45 Minutes
Cook Time: 20 Minutes

Ingredients:
For dough:
2 ½ cups all-purpose flour
1 ½ teaspoon carom seeds
4 teaspoons softened ghee
2 teaspoons salt
Water as needed to make firm yet pliable dough (add teaspoon at a time)

For filling:
Ghee as needed
5-6 medium golden potatoes boiled, peeled, dried, cubed
½ cup frozen peas
1 tablespoon coriander seeds
1 tablespoon pomegranate seeds
1 tablespoon cumin seeds
1 teaspoon dry mango powder
2 teaspoons garam masala
2 teaspoons salt

Instructions:
1. Make dough by combining all ingredients, and set aside to rest under damp towel for 30 minutes.
2. Dry roast coriander, pomegranate, and cumin seeds, then crush with mortar pestle.
3. Then in a wok, add teaspoon of ghee, crushed seeds, and when fragrant, add potatoes and frozen peas.
4. Stir thoroughly, then add dry powder seasoning.
5. Taste and adjust seasoning accordingly.
6. You MUST let potato mixture cool completely before you start your samosas.
7. Flour a dry surface, pinch a golf ball size amount of dough and roll out to oval shape (add flour to the pin to make it easier, and rotate every 4 rolls so that it doesn't stick to the surface).
8. Cut the oval in half, and then wrap into cone shape, pinching the seam to seal completely.
9. Fill generously with potato mixture and then pinch ends together to close into triangle shape.
10. Heat oil on medium low for 10 minutes, then drop a pinch of dough in- If it sizzles, oil is ready. If it sizzles and floats and causes foam, the oil is too hot (listen, I didn't measure the temperature of the oil, I got instructions from a bunch of Indian women. Do you think they use a thermometer? Nope).
11. Drop samosas in (do not crowd) the oil, and flip after five minutes, remove after ten when a dark brown crust has formed.
12. Dry on a paper towel lined plate.

***

Nisha Sharma is the author of the critically acclaimed YA novel *My So-Called Bollywood Life* and the follow up, *Radha and Jai's Recipe for Romance*. She also writes adult contemporary romances including The Singh Family Trilogy and If Shakespeare was an Aunty Trilogy (Launching January 2022). Her writing has been praised by NPR, *Cosmopolitan* Magazine, *Teen Vogue*, Buzzfeed, Hypable and more.

Artichoke Parmesan Dip
Sarah Andre

This is my late uncle's recipe and I recall making a pig-at-a-trough display of myself the first time I tasted this. A food allergy later in life has deprived me of enjoying it, but I continue to make it for parties and it's the first dip that disappears. Enjoy!

Ingredients
 1C mayo (not Miracle Whip)
 1 C shredded parmesan cheese
 14 oz can of artichoke hearts, drained and finely chopped
 1 T lemon juice
 ¼ t pepper

Directions
1. Preheat oven to 400°
2. Mix all ingredients together and bake for 20 minutes. Serve with chunks of sourdough (get a sourdough boule and cut out the center to make a bowl for the dip!)

Boyos
Stacy Finz

This is a savory pastry popular with Sephardic Jews that goes back generations in my family. There are only about 80,000 Sephardic Jews in the United States. Most of my relatives came here from Turkey, where they went to live in 1492, after being expelled from Spain during the Spanish Inquisition. When they left, they took their traditions, language and food with them. I inherited mostly the latter, as well as the possibility that I might be related to singer Neil Sedaka, also a Sephardic Jew and a source of great pride for my grandfather. We make boyos and borekas (see following recipe) for pretty much any family gathering, special occasion and holiday, except of course for Passover, which restricts leavened foods for eight days. Boyos look like pinwheels and are perfect finger foods at parties.

Ingredients:
 1 package puff pastry sheets
 24 ounces feta cheese
 2 to 4 tablespoons minced parsley
 -- Freshly ground black pepper, to taste
 4 eggs
 -- Flour for dusting
 3 tablespoons sesame seeds, or more to taste (optional)

Instructions:

1. Thaw the puff pastry sheets according to package directions.
2. Meanwhile, make the filling. Crumble and mash the feta cheese. Stir in the parsley and pepper. Add 3 of the eggs, one at a time, mashing into the cheese until it takes on a paste-like consistency. Set aside.
3. Remove one sheet of puff pastry and lay on a lightly floured work surface. Using a rolling pin, roll out the sheet until it is about 16 square inches. Cut the sheet into four equal squares. Cut each piece vertically into 4 strips. There will be 16 strips from each sheet of dough. Repeat with remaining sheet.
4. Preheat oven to 350°. Lightly oil a baking sheet.
5. Lightly dust the work surface with flour again. Take one of the strips of puff pastry dough and roll out into a rectangle approximately 10 inches by 3 inches. Spread 2-3 teaspoons of the filling along one of the long edges of the rectangle. Starting at the edge with the filling spread on it, roll the dough toward the other long edge. Then, starting at one end, roll the dough into a spiral shape. Use a little water to attach the end of the dough to itself. Turn it upside down and place it on the baking sheet. The pastries will spread a little while baking, so leave a couple of inches of space between boyos on the sheet. Repeat with the remaining strips.
6. When ready to bake, beat the remaining egg with 1-2 tablespoons of cold water. Brush the tops of the boyos with the egg wash. Sprinkle with sesame seeds (if using) and brush again with the egg wash.
7. Bake until golden brown, about 35-40 minutes.

Makes 32 boyos

Per boyo: 150 calories, 5 g protein, 8 g carbohydrate, 11 g fat (4 g saturated), 45 mg cholesterol, 284 mg sodium, 0 fiber.

Borekas
Stacy Finz

This is a traditional Sephardic savory pastry based on a Finz family recipe. These are stuffed with mashed potatoes. But you can also fill them with meat or vegetables. My grandmother used to make them from rote, eschewing that crazy thing called measurements. So, for years my sister watched her in order to craft a recipe that we could all use and eventually hand down. Like a sandwich or a Cornish pastie, they're portable and make a great finger food at parties or a hearty side dish.

The cheese-mashed potatoes
>   1 pound russet potatoes, peeled and quartered
>   -- Kosher salt
>   1/4 cup heavy cream
>   2 tablespoons unsalted butter
>   -- Freshly ground black pepper, to taste
>   1/2 cup grated Parmesan cheese
>   1 egg, lightly beaten

The pastry
>   1 cup canola oil
>   2 teaspoons kosher salt, or more to taste
>   3 1/2 to 4 cups all-purpose flour
>   1 egg, lightly beaten with 1 tablespoon cold water
>   1/2 cup grated Parmesan cheese

For the potatoes:

1. Place potatoes in a medium pot and cover with cold, salted water. Boil potatoes until cooked through and tender for mashing, about 15-20 minutes. Drain water from pot. Add cream to the pot of potatoes and mash with a hand-held potato masher. Fold in butter and season to taste with salt and pepper. Add Parmesan cheese and egg to potato mixture and fold until completely incorporated. Set aside.
2. Preheat oven to 350°.
3. For the pastry: Add oil, 2/3 water and salt to a small saucepan and stir over medium heat. When the ingredients are fully combined and the liquid starts bubbling, pour the oil mixture into a large mixing bowl and slowly add the flour, 1/2 cup at a time, until you are able to roll the dough in your hands without it sticking.
4. Pinch off golf ball-size pieces of the dough and roll into a ball. Place on a lightly floured surface and with a rolling pin, roll out balls to 4-inch circles. Spoon 1 1/2 teaspoons of the mashed potatoes on one half of the circle, leaving a 1/4-inch border around the edges. Fold the unfilled half of the circle over the filling to form a crescent. Press the seam together with the tines of a fork to seal the pastry.
5. Brush the top of each boreka with the egg wash. Sprinkle the top with cheese. Repeat with remaining dough.
6. Bake on ungreased cookie sheets for 20-25 minutes or until golden brown.

Makes 30 borekas

***

Stacy Finz is a New York Times and USA Today bestselling author of contemporary small-town romance. After more than twenty years covering notorious serial killers, naked-tractor-driving farmers, fanatical foodies, aging rock stars and weird Western towns as a newspaper reporter, she figured she finally had enough material to launch a career writing fiction. She is the author of the Nugget Romance series, the

Garner Brothers series, and the upcoming Dry Creek Ranch series. She lives in Northern California with her husband. Visit her website www.stacyfinz.com.

Chapter Four
Main Dishes

MOM'S ITALIAN STYLE MEAT SAUCE

J. Kenner

I grew up with a single mom who worked full-time, so I was the stereotypical latch-key kid. My mom was often tired, so most evenings, we ate at the television, often on TV trays with TV dinners (back when they had to be heated in the oven!).

But every once in a while, usually on a Friday and *always* on my birthday, my mom would make my favorite meal — spaghetti and meat sauce. Honestly, I really just wanted the meat sauce. It was sooooo yummy, and I would always eat way too much!

When I went off to college, she put the recipe in a graduation-gift recipe binder for me, and I still have that typed, yellowed notecard. I make the meal for my kids now, and it's their favorite too. (And it is also FABULOUS inside an omelet!)

The spice amounts are only until you know the recipe. I don't measure anything anymore. (And I always double the recipe). Basically, this is a fabulous, unbreakable recipe. I hope you enjoy!

Ingredients

2T olive oil
1 onion, diced
2 cloves garlic, crushed
1 lb ground beef
½ green pepper, diced
½ lb mushrooms, diced
1 T. chopped fresh parsley or 1 t. dried
1 #3 can Italian Style Tomatoes*
1 8oz can tomato sauce
1 4oz can tomato paste
1 t. salt

½ t. pepper
1/8 t. red pepper
¼ t. allspice
½ t. oregano
1 t. basil
1 bay leave
1 t sugar (I always leave this out)

*I have no idea what a #3 can is. I just go with a can....
I also sometimes add in a can of stewed tomatoes.

Directions
1. In a 5-6 quart heavy pan, heat oil and sauté onions with garlic lightly.
2. Add meat. Brown meat, stirring to break up pieces.
3. Add green pepper/mushrooms to meat. Cook 2 mins.
4. Stir in other ingredients. Cover and cook 2 hours over low heat. Taste & adjust seasonings.

Serves 4-6; enough to cover 1 lb of spaghetti.

***

J. Kenner (aka Julie Kenner) is the New York Times, USA Today, Publishers Weekly, Wall Street Journal and #1 International bestselling author of over seventy novels, novellas and short stories in a variety of genres.

Though known primarily for her award-winning and internationally bestselling romances (including the Stark and Most Wanted series) that have reached as high as #2 on the New York Times bestseller list and #1 internationally, JK has been writing full time for over a decade in a variety of genres including paranormal and contemporary romance, "chicklit" suspense, urban fantasy, and paranormal mommy lit.

JK has been praised by Publishers Weekly as an author with a "flair for dialogue and eccentric characterizations" and by RT Bookclub for having "cornered the market on sinfully attractive, dominant antiheroes and the women who swoon for them." A four time finalist for Romance Writers of America's prestigious RITA award, JK took home the first RITA trophy in 2014 for her novel, Claim Me (book 2 of her Stark Trilogy).

In her previous career as an attorney, JK worked as a clerk on the Fifth Circuit Court of Appeals, and practiced primarily civil, entertainment and First Amendment litigation in Los Angeles and Irvine, California, as well as in Austin, Texas. She currently lives in Central Texas, with her husband, two daughters, and two rather spastic cats.

Maryland Crab Cakes
Tracey Livesay

I was born in Baltimore and we take our seafood seriously. Whenever there was a family gathering, someone was tasked with buying and bringing a bushel of crabs. You'd clear off a table, spread out a stack of newspapers and go to town. Eating crabs from the shell was tricky to me as a kid; there were parts you could and couldn't eat and I never could figure out which parts would "make me sick." Some of my favorite memories involve sitting next to a grownup who'd crack open the shell and feed me all of the tender, delicious meat. Later, my grandmother would make crab cakes from the leftover crab meat. Watching my grandmother cook was magical, but exact she was not. When I'd ask how much of anything to put into the dish, her response would be, "A little of this," or "A handful," or "A couple of sprinkles." Over the years, from memories, my own research and other recipes, I figured out the amounts and portions until I had a written recipe that was grandmother-approved.

Ingredients
1 egg
1/4 cup mayo
1 TBSP chopped fresh parsley
2 tsp Dijon mustard
2 tsp Worcestershire sauce
1 1/2 tsp Old Bay seasoning
1 tsp fresh lemon juice
1/8 tsp salt
1 pound of fresh lump crab meat
2/3 cup saltine crackers crumbs
2 TBSP melted butter

Directions

1. Whisk the egg, mayo, parsley, Worcestershire sauce, Old Bay, lemon juice and salt together in a large bowl. Place the crab meat on top of the mixture, followed by the cracker crumbs and gently fold all ingredients together. Remember, gently.
2. Cover tightly and refrigerate for at least 30 minutes and no longer than 24 hours.
3. Preheat oven to 450 degrees. Spray baking sheet with nonstick spray.
4. Portion crab cake mixture into even portions on the baking sheet. If you want 6 large crab cakes, use a 1/2 cup measuring cup; for 12 crab cakes, use a 1/4 cup measuring cup; for 24 mini crab puffs, use 2 TBSP size portions. Note that baking time may be shorter for the mini size cakes.
5. Brush the tops of each cake with melted butter.
6. Bake 12-14 minutes until cakes are lightly browned around the edges and on the top.

** Cover leftover crab cakes tightly and refrigerate for up to 5 days or freeze up to 3 months.

** You can freeze the portioned, unbaked crab cakes for up to 3 months. Thaw in the refrigerator, brush with the melted butter, then bake as directed.

***

Tracey Livesay is the acclaimed and award-winning author of sexy and emotional interracial contemporary romances where strong, successful heroines find love with powerful, passionate heroes. A former criminal defense attorney, Tracey lives in Virginia with her husband and three children.

Spinach Fritada (Vegetarian)
Stacy Finz

This is a recipe that has been in my family for generations. It's a Jewish Sephardic cheese dish that's served for desayuno (breakfast) or brunch. Fritada sounds fancy, but it was actually an excuse for my grandmother to use up all the odds and ends of cheese in her refrigerator, usually the last crumbles of feta. She also used cottage cheese and ricotta. Over the years my family has tweaked it a bit. It's easy to make and can be served hot or at warm room temperature. You can even make it ahead and reheat the next day.

Ingredients
    1 tablespoon olive oil
    6 tablespoons dry bread crumbs
    2 16-ounce packages chopped frozen spinach, defrosted
    2 pounds ricotta cheese
    32 ounces low-fat cottage cheese
    7 ounces feta cheese
    4 large eggs
    -- Kosher salt and fresh ground pepper, to taste
    5 ounces Parmesan cheese, shredded or grated

Instructions:
1. Preheat the oven to 350°.

2. Spread the olive oil on the bottom of a 13- by 9- by 2-inch ovenproof baking pan; sprinkle with about 2 tablespoons of bread crumbs. Put the pan in the oven with the door slightly ajar and bake until the crumbs are a golden brown, about 5 minutes.

3. Meanwhile, drain the spinach well, then place in a clean towel and wring firmly to remove as much water as possible. Place the spinach in a large mixing bowl along with the ricotta, cottage cheese and feta cheese; combine well and season to taste with salt and pepper.

4. Whisk the eggs in a separate bowl; add to the spinach-cheese mixture and mix well.

5. Remove the casserole dish from the oven and pour the spinach mixture over the bread crumbs, spreading evenly. Sprinkle top with the Parmesan and remaining 4 tablespoons of bread crumbs. Bake until brown on top and firm, about 1 hour.

Serves 8-10

***

Stacy Finz is a *New York Times* and *USA Today* bestselling author of contemporary small-town romance. After more than twenty years covering notorious serial killers, naked-tractor-driving farmers, fanatical foodies, aging rock stars and weird Western towns as a newspaper reporter, she figured she finally had enough material to launch a career writing fiction. She is the author of the Nugget Romance series, the Garner Brothers series, and the upcoming Dry Creek Ranch series. She lives in Northern California with her husband.

Bleu Cheese Pasta
Nikki Brock

If it's got bleu cheese in it, my husband is all in. This is his favorite recipe. Adjust the bleu cheese to your taste.

Ingredients:
3 pieces bacon
¾ c. onion
1 red bell pepper
½ tsp. fennel seed, crushed
½ tsp. thyme
¼ tsp. pepper
¼ tsp white pepper
red pepper flakes to taste
½ c. chicken broth
3-4 cloves garlic
1 T. salt
¾ c. heavy cream
2 oz. bleu cheese
1 T. parmesan cheese

Directions:
1. Cook bacon in large skillet; break into pieces and set aside. Pour off all but about 1 tablespoon bacon grease.
2. Brown onion and red pepper in grease, then add garlic, black and white peppers, thyme, fennel, and red pepper flakes. Let aromas bloom; add chicken broth.
3. Meanwhile, bring a large pot of water to a boil; add 1 tablespoon salt. Cook pasta until al dente.

4. Pour mixture into blender; blend until almost smooth, then pour back into skillet.
5. Add cream and bleu cheese and stir until melted. Serve over cooked pasta and top with parmesan cheese.

***

Nikki Brock grew up in Tennessee narrating her life in one form or another. Not believing she could become a Real Life Writer (who does that?), she married her real life hero, moved to the Midwest, programmed computers, marketed for an accounting firm, became a graduate student taught in college, moved to the Northeast, and then became a mom. The wife and mom gigs were by far the best. But she never stopped composing stories in her head, and one day she actually wrote one down. When not writing she can be found drinking coffee, the elixir of life, going to estate sales, or binge-watching television shows involving British accents. She loves to read anything and nurses an unhealthy obsession with containers of all sizes. She lives in the Mississippi Delta with her real life hero, two wonderful sons, and two lovely and talented dogs in a diva of an old house that always needs something involving writing checks and which is home to a ghost who smokes.

ENCHILADA CASSEROLE
Sharon Sala

I first had the recipe at a church dinner. I was in my early 20s, so I've had this recipe at least 50 years. I asked for the recipe from the lady who brought the dish and she happily shared it. It has become a huge family favorite, making appearances at family reunions, at holiday dinners, and a food I have taken to neighbors over the years during their illnesses and grief. And every time I make it, I think of the lady who gave it to me, and what an impact that simple gesture has made on the countless lives of others when I shared it, as she shared it with me.

Preheat oven to 375 degrees.

Spray LARGE casserole dish with cooking spray.
You need a large DEEP dish, not a shallow one or it will all bubble over.

Ingredients
  2 pounds of hamburger meat
  1 large onion
  2 cans of Mild Enchilada Sauce (I use Old El Paso and you can go hotter on the choices)
  2 cans of Cream of Mushroom soup
  1 LARGE and one medium bag of plain Doritos corn chips. Not flavored.
  2 cups of grated cheese (at least)

Instructions

1. Cook hamburger meat and diced onion together until done but not browned. Add Enchilada Sauce and stir. turn off the heat and set aside.
2. Heat 2 cans of cream of mushroom soup with 2 cans of water until hot and well blended.
3. Crush the bags of Doritos. Just open the top and crush inside the bag.
4. Begin by layering meat on the bottom, then add crushed chips, then pour some of the mushroom soup on that, then sprinkle some cheese.
5. Repeat layers until they're gone. Add a good layer of the grated cheese on top, cover with a lid and bake at 375 degrees for about 45 minutes.

If my casserole dish looks pretty full, I usually set it ON a cookie sheet so if it bubbles over it won't make a mess in the bottom of the stove.

SMOTHERED CHICKEN
Sharon Sala

Every time I make this, I think of my mother and my grandmother. They were the best at smothering tenderized steaks, and cuts of chicken, and pork chops. The gravy made from the mushroom soup is perfect, and cooking it with those cuts of meat is the ultimate topping for mashed potatoes. Sometimes we would have a vegetable as a side, and sometimes we'd just add a tossed salad. But chicken cooked this way is fork tender and truly falls off the bone. Just thinking about it makes my mouth water. A food from my childhood that I share with you.

Preheat oven to 400 degrees

Grease a large casserole dish

Ingredients
   1 whole 2-3 lb chicken, cut into pieces as if you were
       going to fry it
   2 cans of cream of mushroom soup
   Milk

Instructions
1. Brown the pieces of chicken and put into a greased casserole pan or a baking pan.
2. Put mushroom soup into a separate pan
3. Use empty soup can for measure and add 2 cans of milk into soup and heat until bubbly.

67

4. Pour over chicken.
5. Cover casserole with lid or aluminum foil and bake for an hour

If you don't want to make that much at once, just use pieces of chicken that you buy separately and only 1 can of mushroom soup and 1 can of milk.

It's great re-heated and can be frozen.

Very easy and very tasty. It's a family favorite.

Add some mashed potatoes, use the mushroom soup from the chicken as your gravy. That and a salad makes a very tasty and hearty meal.

***

Sharon Sala is a native Oklahoman and still lives within a two-hour drive of where she was born. First published in 1991, she is a New York Times/USA Today best-selling author with a 132 plus books published in seven different genres, including Romantic Suspense, Mystery, Young Adult, Western, Fiction, Women's Fiction, and Non-Fiction.

Industry Awards include:
  Eight-time RITA Finalist (Romance Industry Award)
  The Janet Dailey Award
  Five-Time Career Achievement winner from RT Magazine
  Five-time winner of the National Reader's Choice Award
  Five-time winner of the Colorado Romance Writer's Award of Excellence
  Heart of Excellence Award
  Booksellers Best Award
  Nora Roberts Lifetime Achievement Award RITA, presented by RWA
  Centennial Award from RWA for recognition of her 100th published novel

With two great grandmothers of Native American descent on her father's side of the family, one belonging to the Cherokee tribe, and the other a member of the Cree tribe, she has followed the path of a storyteller, and considers it her gift from Spirit.

Most of her stories come first to her as dreams, which then become the books she writes. She dreams in color, with dialogue, and when she writes, she sees the scenes in her head as a movie playing out before her.

Writing changed her life, her world, and her fate.

Bulgogi (Korean grilled beef)
JoAnn Brown

Two of my children were born in Korea, so I wanted to learn to cook some Korean specialties that we'd enjoyed in restaurants. Not *kimchee*, the pickled cabbage and peppers that takes up to six months to ferment and is a special recipe handed down from mother to daughter. I decided to try bulgogi. The first time I made it, I called my husband and asked, "Is it supposed to smell like skunk when it's marinating?" The sesame oil has a strong scent that reminded me of that odor when it was first poured out. The smell quickly dissipates and leaves the meat with a wonderful flavor. After that, the children loved to reply when friends asked what was for supper, "We're having skunk meat." This is a sweet, flavorful beef that you can grill or broil. We broiled it until we realized Korean friends threw it on the grill which gives it a flavor closer to the authentic dish which is cooked at the table around a tube filled with charcoal. It's our Fourth of July meal, combining our children's national dish and the holiday that's become synonymous with backyard grills.

This recipe can be easily doubled/tripled/cut by one third/whatever you need. This version serves four.

Ingredients
3 lbs of beef – London broil or top round works best–thinly sliced or cut into 1" chunks
½ cup brown sugar
1½ cups of soy sauce

Black pepper to taste

3 tablespoons of roasted sesame seeds

3/4 cup sesame oil

1½ tablespoons of chopped/minced garlic (add more or less depending on how much you like garlic)

2 medium sized onions, peeled and quartered and separated into individual pieces

Instructions

1. Mix all ingredients together in a large nonporous bowl. Cover with foil or lid.
2. Let marinate in the refrigerator for a minimum of 4 hours, stirring every hour or so to get all the meat into the marinade
3. Put foil on your grill/broiler. Place meat and onions on the foil and grill until thoroughly cooked. Throw out marinade.
4. Remove meat and onions and serve. We usually have fried rice with it. If you want to be really authentic, serve with white rice and *banchan* (small dishes of pickled vegetables or bean sprouts).

***

JoAnn Brown has published over 100 titles under a variety of pen names. A former military officer, she enjoys taking pictures and traveling. She has taught creative writing for more than 20 years and is always excited when one of her students sells a project. She has been married for more than 40 years and has three children and two rambunctious cats. She lives in Amish Country in southeastern Pennsylvania.

Salmon Bake
Valerie Clarizio

This recipe came from my brother who is a professional fisherman and is a winter go-to meal for us. My husband and I fish with him frequently, so I can quite a bit of salmon. My romance author logo is on the side of my brother's boat and on his jersey. How many professional fishermen can say they are sponsored by a romance writer?

Ingredients
½ C Mayonnaise
½ C Bread Crumbs
1 Egg
½ Red Pepper
½ Medium Size Onion
1 Tbsp Garlic Powder
1 Tbsp Cayenne Pepper
Dash of Paprika
Dash of Lemon Juice
1 Pint of Canned Salmon

Combine all the ingredients and mix well. Flatten into a 9 X 13 greased, glass pan. Bake at 350 degrees for 25-30 minutes.

***

Valerie Clarizio is a USA Today Bestselling author who lives in romantic Door County Wisconsin with her husband. She's an outdoors enthusiast, of which her favorite activity is hiking in national parks. While out on the trails, she has plenty of time to conjure up irresistible characters and unique storylines for her next romantic suspense or sweet contemporary romance novel.

Baked Ziti
Gemma Brocato

Who doesn't love a gooey, cheesy dish of pasta? If you glanced at my waistline, you'd know I never pass up a plate. But I will modify a recipe to try to make it healthier as I've done with this recipe. Ziti is one of my go-to comfort foods.

Ingredients
3 cups (about 8 oz) of Ziti, uncooked
3 cups (28 oz) of spaghetti sauce – I use a fairly good quality sauce
1 large can (28 oz) diced tomatoes with sauce
1 ¾ cup (15 oz) of low-fat ricotta cheese
2 cups (8 oz) of part skim shredded mozzarella cheese, divided
1 tsp dried basil
¼ tsp ground black pepper, or more to taste
Grated parmesan cheese
Optional add-ins:
Cooked, crumbled Italian sausage, sweet or spicy
Green onions, to taste
Frank's Hot Sauce, because we put that on a lot of things

Directions
1. Heat oven to 350º.
2. Cook pasta according to package directions. Drain.
3. Combine spaghetti sauce and tomatoes in a large bowl. (Add the sausage or green onions here is you are using.)
4. In another bowl, combine ricotta cheese, 1 cup of the mozzarella, and the seasoning. (Add the Frank's to this mixture if you use it.)
5. Toss hot, drained pasta with the spaghetti/tomato mixture.
6. In a 9 x 13 baking dish, spoon ½ of the pasta mixture, then top with cheese mixture. Then cover with the remaining pasta.
7. Sprinkle the remaining mozzarella and parmesan cheese.
8. Cover loosely with foil. Bake 25 minutes.
9. Remove foil and bake another 5 minutes until the dish is hot and bubbly.

One Pan Salmon and Brussels Sprouts
Gemma Brocato

I'm sharing this recipe which my lovely daughter created because I'm so proud of the chef she has become. And because after a busy day of doing life, sometimes, things should be as easy as one pan meals. Cheers, Erin!

Ingredients
2-4 salmon fillets, about 4 oz each
Extra virgin olive oil
Salt
Pepper
Panko breadcrumbs*
½ tsp dill weed
Brussels sprouts
1 tbsp Extra virgin olive oil
1 tbsp Balsamic vinegar
1 ½ tsp maple syrup
Crumbled bacon about 2-3 cooked slices will do. (Optional for vegetarians)

Directions
1. Line a baking sheet with foil, and top with parchment.
2. Brush salmon fillets with EVOO and season with salt and pepper. Arrange on one half of the prepared baking sheet.
3. Mix breadcrumbs and dill together, then top each fillet.
4. Trim the Brussels sprouts and slice in half.
5. Toss with more EVOO, the balsamic vinegar and maple syrup.

6. Add crumbled bacon, if using.
7. Spread the sprouts on the other side of the pan with the salmon.
8. Preheat oven to 400º.
9. Bake 15-20 minutes, tossing the Brussels sprouts halfway through baking.

*My daughter found gluten-free breadcrumbs and uses those.

Stuffed Poblanos
K.D. Garcia

Ingredients

6 medium poblanos sliced in halves and roasted with skin and seeds removed*

2 tablespoons olive oil

1 green bell pepper

1 white onion

2 cloves fresh garlic

1 ½ pounds of ground beef or turkey

5-6 plum tomatoes roasted with skin off* and chopped

1 - 15 oz can black beans drained

1 - 15 oz can corn drained

2 tsp granulated tomato bullion

1 tsp cumin

1 tsp coriander

salt and pepper to taste

2 cups Chihuahua cheese

Adobo salsa

Before you start working with the chilis, put on gloves and never, ever touch your eyes.

Instructions

1. To roast the vegies, set the oven on broil. Line a cookie sheet with aluminum foil and spray with cooking spray. Cut tomatoes, jalapenos, or poblanos into two halves. Scoop out and discard

seeds from the peppers. Place the cut side down on the sheet and spray a light coat of cooking spray on the tops of the vegies. Put in oven and roast for 10-15 minutes, until the skin bubbles away from the vegetable. Remove from the oven, wrap in a moist paper towel, and let sit until cooled. Once it's cooled, the skin should pull away easily.

2. Set oven to 350^0 F.

3. Warm olive oil in a large skillet. Add the bell pepper, onion, and garlic. Cook until soft. Set aside. In the same skillet, brown the ground beef. Pour off any grease and return the bell pepper, and onion to the skillet. Add the tomatoes, black beans, corn, bullion, cumin, coriander, salt, and pepper. Heat through and divide stuffing evenly among peppers. Sprinkle with Chihuahua cheese and cook for 15 to 20 minutes, until the cheese has melted. Serve with adobo salsa.

Khichuri
Meredith Bond

On cold, wet rainy days of Fall, there's nothing like a hot bowl of something thick and yummy to warm you up. Well, in Bengal, India (where my husband was born and raised), that hot, yummy something is a mush of rice, lentils and vegetables called khichuri. It's eaten with fried foods – usually a fried egg or omelet, papad (lentil snacks) and fried potatoes (my mother-in-law makes French fries to die for).

It doesn't take too long, although it does require some pretty constant watching to be sure there's enough water so that it doesn't burn on the bottom of your pot. But believe me, it's well worth the stirring.

Ingredients:
- 1 cup rice
- 1 cup split red lentils (Masoor dal)
- 4 cups water to start
- 2 cups cauliflower cut into small pieces
- 2 small red potatoes, cut into chunks
- 1 whole small onion
- ¼ tsp turmeric
- 1 tsp cumin
- ¼ tsp coriander
- ½ tsp ginger paste
- ¼ tsp sugar
- 1 tsp salt

Spice mixture (for the end):
- 1 small onion sliced thin
- 1 Tbs butter or ghee
- 2 bay leaves
- 1-2 dried red chilies

2 cinnamon sticks
2 cardamom pods
3 cloves

Directions:

1. Boil 4 cups of water in a large pot. Add in rice and dal over medium heat, covered, and let cook for 10 minutes until it's about half done. Watch to see it doesn't boil over.
2. Stir in spices, including salt and sugar. Let cook for another 5 minutes.
3. Add in the cauliflower and potatoes and the whole onion (which you can slice in half if you think it's too big). Let cook at medium-low heat, adding water as necessary to keep the consistency from getting too thick (halfway between soup and paste, more like a stew consistency). Stir every now and then to check it isn't sticking to the bottom.
4. While that's cooking, in a separate frying pan, melt the butter over medium-high heat. Add in the spices of the spice mixture listed above.
5. After the aroma of the spices has come out, add in the onion and fry together, stirring occasionally, until the onion is soft and golden (7-8 minutes).
6. When the potatoes are soft in the khichuri, add in the spice mixture and blend well.
7. Remove from heat and serve with your fried egg/fries/papad. If you have an Indian grocery near by, pick up a bottle of sweet lime or mango pickle (like Major Gray's Chutney) to eat with your khichuri. It adds a wonderful sweet-sour flavor.

Enjoy and stay warm!

***

Meredith Bond's books straddle that beautiful line between historical romance and fantasy. An award-winning author, she writes fun, traditional Regency romances, medieval Arthurian romances, and Regency romances with a touch of magic. Known for her characters "who slip readily into one's heart," Meredith loves to take her readers on a journey they won't soon forget. She is currently living in Europe enjoying the Bohemian life.

West Texas–Style Cumin–Pepper Steak Tacos
Lori Wilde

Growing up in West Texas, tacos was the meal my four siblings and I most looked forward to. My folks were schoolteachers and we didn't have much money for luxuries, so taco night came just once a month on pay day. Here are two of the recipes my mother used.

Ingredients:
 2 pounds flat-iron steaks
 Olive oil, for drizzling
 1 rounded tablespoon ground cumin
 2 teaspoons granulated garlic
 2 teaspoons granulated onion
 ½ teaspoon chili powder
 2 tablespoons fresh thyme, chopped or 1 teaspoon ground thyme
 Salt and pepper
 2 limes

For the Peppers and Onions:
 2 tablespoons canola or olive oil
 1 large red bell or frying pepper, sliced
 1 large green frying, mild or bell pepper, sliced
 1 large red onion, halved and sliced
 4 cloves garlic, sliced
 Salt and pepper

Directions:
1. Bring the steaks to room temperature and coat lightly in olive or canola oil. Combine cumin, granulated garlic and onion, thyme, salt and pepper in a small bowl and rub into the meat. Let stand covered for 30 minutes.
2. Heat a griddle or grill pan to medium high heat for steaks.
3. Heat large skillet with canola or olive oil, 2 turns of the pan. Add red and green mild peppers, red onions and garlic, and season with salt and pepper. Cook veggies to tender-crisp, 4-5 minutes, deglaze the pan with sherry or white wine.
4. Grill steaks for 8 minutes turning once for medium rare, 10-12 minutes for medium-well. Grill 2 halved limes alongside steaks. Let steaks rest and thinly slice on angle against the grain. Douse meat with juice of grilled limes. Assemble lettuce or tacos as you like.

Fixins': Sliced Radishes, cilantro, avocado or guacamole, sour cream or Mexican crema, shredded cheese.

Pork Carnitas
(Slow Cooker Pulled Pork Tacos)
Lori Wilde

Since the slow-cooker tacos took longer to make, Mom would put a large batch in the crock-pot on Sunday morning before church and make flour tortillas when we got home. We'd eat on them for days until all the meat was gone. The following is a downsized version of her recipe.

Ingredients:
4-5 lb boneless pork shoulder, skinless
2 tablespoons salt
1 teaspoon black pepper
1 onion, chopped
2 jalapenos, deseeded, chopped
1 serrano pepper, deseeded, chopped
4 cloves garlic, minced
2 oranges, juice only

Rub
2 tablespoon dried oregano
4 teaspoon ground cumin
2-3 tbsp olive oil

Directions:
1. Dry the pork shoulder and rub with salt and pepper.
2. Combine the rub ingredients then rub all over the pork.
3. Place the pork in a slow cooker (fat cap up), top with the onion, jalapeño, serrano, minced garlic (don't worry about spreading it) and squeeze over the juice of the oranges.

81

4. Slow Cook on low for 9-10 hours or on high for 6 hours.
5. Pork should be tender enough to shred. Remove from slow cooker and let cool slightly. Then shred using two forks.
6. Optional: Skim off the fat from the juices remaining in the slow cooker and discard.
7. If you have a lot more than 2 cups of juice, then reduce it down to about 2 cups. The liquid will be salty, it is the seasoning for the pork. Set liquid aside – do not bother straining onion etc, it's super soft.

To Crisp:

1. Heat 1 tbsp of oil in a large nonstick pan or well-seasoned skillet over high heat. Spread pork in the pan, drizzle some of your juices over top. Wait until the juices evaporate and the bottom side is golden brown and crusty. Turn and just briefly sear the other side – you don't want to make it brown all over because then it's too crispy, need tender juicy bits.
2. Remove pork from skillet. Repeat in batches (takes me 4 batches) – don't crowd the pan.
3. Just before serving, drizzle over more juices and serve hot, stuffed in tacos

***

Lori Wilde is an award-winning, New York Times, USA Today, and Publishers' Weekly bestselling author of 96 works of romantic fiction. Her books have been translated into 26 languages, with more than four million copies of her books sold worldwide. Her breakout novel, The First Love Cookie Club, has been optioned for a TV movie, as well as her Wedding Veil Wishes series.

Lori is a registered nurse with a BSN from Texas Christian University. She holds a certificate in forensics and is also a certified yoga instructor. A fifth-generation Texan, Lori lives with her husband, Bill, in the Cutting Horse Capital of the World; where they run Epiphany Orchards, a writing/creativity retreat for the care and enrichment of the artistic soul.

Fish and Potato Pie
Toni Anderson

As a former Marine Biologist, I feel like I have to include a fish dish! This is a very simple but extremely tasty meal and goes well with sides of green peas or steamed asparagus. I like to use smoked haddock if I can get it, but you can use a mixture of any tasty smoked fish (try to avoid anything too bony). This recipe makes me miss living on the coast. One day I'll get back there-maybe I'll get my dream writing room with an ocean view.

INGREDIENTS:
    450g/1 lb new potatoes
    50g/2 oz butter
    100g/4 oz mushrooms, cleaned and sliced
    450g/1 lb smoked haddock fillets, skinned and
        flaked (or any smoked fish)
    1 (227g/8oz) can chopped tomatoes
    150ml/ ¼ pint sour cream
    50g/2 oz mature cheddar cheese, grated
    Fresh parsley to garnish.

DIRECTIONS:
1. Wash and steam/boil the potatoes until just tender, 15-20 minutes (depending on size).
2. Cool and cut them into thick slices.
3. Use a little butter to lightly grease a casserole dish and arrange a layer of sliced potatoes on the bottom.
4. Mix the fish, mushrooms and tomatoes with

their juice into a large bowl, add the sour cream and combine well. Tip this mixture on top of the initial potato layer, then arrange another layer of potatoes on top.

5. Dot with butter and add the grated cheese.
6. Bake in a moderate oven (180C, 350F, Gas 4) for 25 to 30 minutes.
7. Garnish with fresh parsley before serving. (Serves 4)

***

Toni Anderson writes gritty, sexy, FBI Romantic Thrillers, and is a New York Times and a USA Today bestselling author. Her books have won the Readers' Choice, Aspen Gold, Book Buyers' Best, Golden Quill, and National Excellence in Romance Fiction awards. She's been a finalist in both the Vivian Contest and the RITA Award from the Romance Writers of America, and also in the Daphne du Maurier Award of Excellence. More than two million copies of her books have been downloaded.

Best known for her "COLD" books perhaps it's not surprising to discover Toni lives in one of the most extreme climates on earth-- Manitoba, Canada. Formerly a Marine Biologist, she still misses the ocean, but is lucky enough to travel for research purposes. In January 2016, she visited FBI Headquarters in Washington DC, including a tour of the Strategic Information and Operations Center. She hopes not to get arrested for her Google searches.

Succulent King Crab Legs
Tracey Devlyn

Every New Year's Eve, I treat my family to a King Crab Leg Feast. This is, by far, the most foolproof recipe I've tried. The meat comes out so tender and flavorful, every time. My husband makes a great show of wrangling the spiky shells until I yank, er, take the legs and crack 'em for him. His grateful smile is worth the thousand tiny puncture wounds to my fingers.

Ingredients
  2 pounds King Crab legs (or snow crab legs)
  ¼ cup apple cider vinegar
  3 tablespoons lemon juice
  1 teaspoon salt
  1 tablespoon Old Bay seafood mix

Directions
1. Defrost crab legs.
2. Fill a large cooking pot with water (enough to cover crab legs).
3. Add apple cider vinegar, lemon juice, salt, and seasoning.
4. Bring water to a boil.
5. Fully submerge crab legs in boiling water.
6. Allow water to boil again (approx. 6 minutes)
7. Once the water begins to boil, turn off heat and cover pan.
8. Let crab legs sit in water for 3-4 minutes.

NOTE: Maximum cook time = 10 minutes, including boiling (6 min) and resting time (4 min). If you cook them any longer, crab legs can lose their tenderness. Sweet spot tends to be 8-9 minutes.

Serve with melted butter (I like to drizzle lemon juice in mine).

Substitute for Old Bay seasoning:
    1 tablespoon celery salt
    1 tablespoon ground bay leaves
    2 teaspoons black pepper
    1 teaspoon paprika
    ½ teaspoon dry mustard
    pinch - cinnamon, nutmeg, and ground cloves

Directions
1. Add all dry ingredients to a small bowl and mix well.

***

USA Today bestselling author **Tracey Devlyn** wanted to be the next Dian Fossey and explore the wilds of Africa, but that was before she met chemistry and calculus and realized a business major, rather than a science degree, might be a better fit.

With an enthusiasm for research that translates into creative (and disturbing) plot twists for her characters to navigate, it's no surprise that her suspense-laden stories excite her readers and offer a glimpse of the nefarious nature lurking behind her sweet smile. Despite the thrilling, emotional ride Tracey gives her readers, she enjoys an annoyingly normal lifestyle with her husband and rescue dogs at her suburban home outside Chicago.

Baked Catfish
Leslie Hachtel

I love fish but I don't like it fried so I came up with this healthier alternative.

Ingredients
    1-1/4 pounds catfish
    Seasoned bread crumbs (you can use regular or gluten-free)
    Paprika

Directions
1. Preheat oven to 350. Cover a cookie sheet with tinfoil and spread out fish. Cover with bread crumbs and then turn over and cover the other side. Sprinkle with paprika to taste.
2. Bake for 40-45 minutes. The edges will be crispy and the fish moist. Enjoy.

***

Leslie Hachtel started writing years ago when she simply decided to sit down at a typewriter and she was transported to another world. She realized then a writer writes because there is no other choice.

She is a bestselling author and her genres include historical, contemporary, romantic suspense and historical/paranormal since she loves them all.

Leslie lives in Florida with her fabulously supportive husband, Bob. And of course, with Josie, the poodle mix.

Chicken Divan
Sarah Andre

Going through my old recipe books for this project has been a lovely walk down memory lane. Mom would make each of us our favorite meal on our birthdays and- yep- you guessed it, this one was mine! Secret: I have not made this for myself since my late 20's (early 1990's!) I'm determined, after all this time, to serve this again next week and once again taste the absolute deliciousness!

Ingredients
2 10 oz pkgs Frozen, chopped broccoli
2 C diced chicken (white meat)
2 C Cream of Chicken soup
1 C mayo
1 t lemon juice
½ t curry powder
½ C shredded cheddar
1 C soft bread cut into small cubes
1 T melted butter

Directions
1. Preheat oven to 350°
2. Partially cook the broccoli and layer the bottom of a greased 9" x 13" baking dish. Add chicken. Combine soup, mayo, lemon juice, and curry. Spoon over the chicken. Sprinkle with cheese. Combine bread cubes with butter and place on top.
3. Bake uncovered for 30 min until cheese is bubbling. Serve over rice.

– Serves 6

Mom's Crock Pot Stew
Jo McNally

Both my mom and dad grew up with very little. Mom knew how to stretch a meal, and Dad knew how to stock the freezer with meat.

You see, Dad had become the "man of the house" when he was just a boy, after his father died young and left a wife and four little children living on a rocky farm in northern New York. My dad was plowing the fields behind a team of horses and hunting for food to support his family by the time he was ten or twelve, and was one of most hard-working, honorable men I ever knew. He was truly, deeply, quietly *good* at heart, and my fictional heroes all have that deep sense of goodness because of my dad. One of my heroes (a father, of course) even carries Dad's middle name--Asher in *Nora's Guy Next Door.*

My mom originally made this delicious stew with venison, but it's excellent with beef, too. She'd brown up the meat and slice the veggies the night before, then put this together in the morning before she went to work. When we came home, the house smelled *amazing!!*

Ingredients:
  6 strips of bacon, cut in ½ inch pieces
  3 lbs beef (stew meat), cut into evenly-sized pieces
  1 large carrot, grated
  1 medium onion, sliced
  3 Tbsp flour

1 10 oz can condensed beef broth
1 Tbsp catsup
½ tsp whole thyme
1 whole bay leaf
1 lb fresh mushrooms, sliced
1 ½ tsp salt (or to taste)
⅛ tsp pepper
2 Tbsp butter
½ cup dry red wine

Directions

1. Cook bacon in large skillet until crisp. Remove and drain.
2. Add beef cubes and brown.
3. Place browned meat in small crock pot.
4. Brown carrots and onion in skillet, season with salt and pepper.
5. Stir in flour.
6. Add broth, mix well and add to crock pot.
7. Add cooked bacon, thyme, catsup and bay leaf.
8. Cover and cook on low 8 to 10 hours.
9. Sauté mushrooms in 2 tablespoons butter and add to crock pot with red wine one hour before serving.
10. Thicken with flour if needed.
11. Serve over egg noodles.

***

Jo McNally lives in upstate New York with 100 pounds of dog and 200 pounds of husband – her slice of the bed is very small. When she's not writing or reading romance novels (or clinging to the edge of the bed...), she can often be found on the back porch sipping wine with friends, listening to an eclectic playlist. If the weather is perfect, she might join her husband on the golf course, where she always feels far more competitive than her actual skill-level would suggest.

Beef Burgundy
Mary K. Tilghman

I first tasted this as a nervous girlfriend meeting my now-husband's family for the first time. I soon discovered it was one of several recipes that my future mother-in-law Mary Angela Truitt counted on for Sunday suppers. She had enjoyed it at a friend's Christmas tree un-trimming and asked for the recipe.

When I became engaged to her son Ray, I was given my own copy and it is that handwritten version I still refer to whenever I make it–usually for Sunday family suppers.

For their April 2021 wedding, my son Sean Truitt and his fiancée Nina asked for a copy of the recipe so their caterer could include it on their buffet. Until then, I had no idea how much our three children loved this recipe.

It's quick and easy. Using good wine will improve the flavor but any dry red wine will do fine.

Ingredients
> 1 pound or more beef chunks cut into bite-sized cubes
> 1 package Lipton Onion Soup mix
> 2 cups dry red wine
> salt and pepper to taste
> 1/4 cup fine bread crumbs
> 1/4 cup flour

Directions
1. Mix breadcrumbs and flour and coat beef cubes.
2. Sprinkle soup mix over beef.
3. Add to casserole pan with wine, salt and pepper.
4. Bake at 300 degrees F for 2-3 hours, depending on depth of baking dish and amount of beef used.
5. Serve with rice, cooked noodles or mashed potatoes.

***

Mary K. Tilghman, a Baltimore native, is author of four novels and seven travel guides.

Homemade Tomato Sauce...
made with a Food Mill
Lucy Farago

I've never been much for canning. One, its time consuming and two, its time consuming.

But as summer approaches, I hear Martha Stuart in my head. I should probably talk to someone about that, but channeling someone else can prove an effective way to let my muse know she'd better get a move on or I'll replace her. Works like a charm.

I suggest purchasing a food mill. You won't regret it after tasting this sauce. If you don't have fresh tomatoes at your fingertips, nothing beats a Sunday afternoon carousing a farmer's market, the aroma of freshly baked goods tempting you to spend your entire budget on assorted pies and breads you wish you had the talent to create. But try not to break the bank and get yourself to the tomato vendor. In the fall, I buy an entire case and split it with my neighbor. We spend a day peeling, bagging and freezing them for the winter. The bottle of wine could be why it's a yearly event, but I suspect good old Martha has something to do with it too. But, I digress. I started milling tomatoes because they'd over-ripe before I ate them. My mother says throw them in a freezer bag for winter soups. That works too but honestly, I prefer this sauce.

Directions
1. Preheat oven to 425 F.
2. Cover a cooking pan–pan, not sheet–with tin foil. It will help with clean up, it won't oxidize your tray, and catches all the beautiful drippings you want in your sauce.
3. After cut in half length wise, you'll require enough ripened*

tomatoes to fill the tray, leaving small gaps between slices. (*deep red and on the soft side, for those of you who don't have a celebrity chef taking up space in your head).

4. You have two choices. Use a large bowl or, lay them directly on the tray for seasoning. Depends how messy you like to get with your hands. But remember, tactile cooking is good for the muse.
5. Season the tomatoes with Kosher salt and fresh ground pepper.
6. Peel and separate half a garlic bulb, ensuring the individual cloves are on the large size. (they're going to bake with the tomatoes so plump cloves provide better flavor)
7. Drizzle olive oil over the tomatoes. (about ¼ cup)
8. You can add several sprigs of fresh basil or oregano if you wish.
9. Toss the tomatoes in the bowl or get down and dirty with your hands. Then flip them sliced side down on the tray. (this will allow the skin to blister and add more flavor)
10. If you like a less sweet sauce, drizzle balsamic glaze on the tomatoes.
11. Cook for at least 25-30 minutes depending on your oven. You'll want everything roasted (wrinkly and toasty brown, even charred, in color). The garlic will turn deep yellow or even green.
12. Remove from oven and let cool for 5 minutes, so as to avoid burning yourself. Then put your food mill over a large bowl and spoon/pour everything on the tin foil into the mill. Crank the mill until you achieve a very dry pulp.

If you don't have a food mill you can...
- gently peel off the skin, if you prefer it off.
- use a blender or an emulsifier
- or use a potato masher if you prefer chunky with seeds.

The sauce is ready to eat, or can be frozen, either in a jar or freezer bags. I never toss tomatoes out. If I don't have enough for a jar, I will opt for my mom's method and bag them in the freezer. But I promise, you'll appreciate this home-made sauce.

***

Lucy Farago knows there is nothing like a happy sigh at the end of a good book. With the encouragement of her loving husband, she wrote her first manuscript. An unpublished historical, it sits in a file on her computer, there to remind her how much fun she had learning the craft and becoming part of an industry whose books make you believe anything is possible. A big fan of Agatha Christie, she set out to write her first romantic suspense novel. Thrilled to be a published author, Lucy also teaches yoga, enjoys cooking, and saying what other people are thinking. In her fantasy world, her beautiful Siberian husky, Loki, doesn't shed and her three kids clean up after themselves. Alas, that fantasy will never see fruition.

Chorizo Zucchini Tacos for Two
Terri Reed

Unlike my writing where I plot heavily, when I cook, I wing it. This recipe is my take on Zucchini Boats which usually are made with Italian flavors, but I wanted to find a low carb way to use chorizo, and this was delicious.

Ingredients
- 1 pound favorite type of ground chorizo- I use a beef and pork combo-either with verde (green chili) or rojo (red chili)
- ¼ cup diced tomatoes
- ¼ cup diced yellow onion
- 1/8 cup chopped cilantro
- 2 tablespoons favorite salsa (you can add more depending on how wet you want the mixture)
- Two Zucchini
- Grated cheese (I like pepper jack but white or orange cheddar would also be tasty)

Directions
1. Heat oven to 400 degrees.
2. Grease a glass pan
3. Cut the ends of the zucchini, then cut lengthwise, then quarter. Gently scoop out the middle of each quarter to make a nice divot. Place in greased glass pan, sprinkle with salt and pepper. Set aside.

4. In a skillet, brown the chorizo.
5. In a bowl, combine ½ cup of the chorizo (the extra chorizo is great in eggs the next day), the diced tomatoes, the onion, cilantro and salsa
6. Stuff the zucchini with the chorizo mixture-put in oven for 20 minutes.
7. At the 20-minute mark, take out of oven and sprinkle cheese (use as little or as much as you'd like)
8. Then put pan back in oven to let the cheese melt. Keep an eye on it and it's okay if the cheese browns a bit.
9. Take out of oven, sprinkle a bit of cilantro on top and let rest for at least five minutes. The zucchini retains the heat, so be careful. When it's cooled enough to your liking, serve. You can cut it up into bite sizes or pick up like a taco. Enjoy!

***

Bestselling, award-winning author **Terri Reed** writes books infused with family and faith. When not writing, she enjoys spending time with her family and friends and agility training with her dog.

The Easiest Chicken You'll Ever Make
Lori Ryan

Okay, let's be real here. I'm a romance writer, wife, and mom of three. I'm an avid reader, too. Sometimes I've got my nose stuck in a book and I don't want to get out of the imaginary world I'm either writing in or reading about.

Problem is, those pesky kids want to be fed. Like, every day. Every single day. Sometimes more than once. If you're reading this recipe book, I know you've been there. This is a great go-to recipe when you need to feed yourself or the fam and you don't want to have to leave that make believe world any longer than necessary.

I don't remember where I first learned this strategy. I'm calling it a strategy because it's honestly more of a strategy than a recipe. I think it was in a Facebook post. Or it might have just been a friend. Hmmmm, seems like it might have been my old assistant. She has kids, too. (Ehlane, if it was you, thank you!)

Ingredients:
    1lb boneless chicken breast or tenders (more or less as needed)
    1 jar fire roasted tomatoes (or pureed/chopped/diced canned tomatoes)
    Some kind of carb to eat it on (cooked rice, rolls, tortillas, pasta, or if you're really up for it and want to make this healthy–cooked veggies like carrots, zucchini, or summer squash)

Directions
Brace yourself. Here it goes.
1. Take the chicken and toss it in a frying pan. Pour the tomatoes over it. Add a little salt. If you want to go nuts, you can add things like garlic or Italian seasoning. I don't. I'm lazy.

2. Put the cover on that and bring the sauce to a boil, then lower it to a simmer and cover the pan. Let that bad boy cook until the chicken is cooked through. The time will depend on how large your chicken pieces are. If they're smaller, it might cook in about 10-15 minutes. Tenders cook fast so watch them. If your pieces are thicker, it might take 30 minutes. I always cut my chicken into chunks and it takes about 20 minutes to cook.

3. When it's finished, you can put it on top of cooked rice or over pasta. You could toast some rolls and make this the stuffing for a messy sandwich. Or, if you need to get some veggies into you or the kiddos, sauté up some veggies and serve this on top.

The cool thing about this is that you can do it a bunch of different ways. You can substitute a jar of pre-made tikka masala sauce from the store and serve this with naan. You can use barbeque sauce and serve it with sliced bread and corn.

So, simmer it up and get yourself back to the book! Your HEA is waiting!

***

Lori Ryan is a NY Times and USA Today bestselling author who writes romantic suspense and contemporary romance with steamy love scenes and characters you won't want to leave in the pages when the story is over.

Lori published her first novel in April of 2013 and has fallen in love with writing. She is the author of the Sutton Capital Series; the Heroes of Evers, Texas; and the Triple Play Curse Novellas, a set of novellas with sexy baseball players at their core as part of Bella Andre's Game For Love Kindle World. She has also published in Melanie Shawn's Hope Falls Kindle World and in Robyn Peterman's Magic and Mayhem Kindle World.

She lives with an extremely understanding husband, three wonderful children, and two mostly well-behaved dogs in Austin, Texas. It's a bit of a zoo, but she wouldn't change a thing.

Spicy Sausage Pasta
Nikki Sloane

This is my family's favorite dish. It's the ultimate comfort food, takes 20 minutes total, and only requires one pot!

Ingredients
- 1 Tbsp olive oil
- 1 lb. smoked sausage
- ½ onion, diced
- 2 cloves of garlic, minced
- 2 cups chicken broth (14.5 oz. can)
- 1 (10 oz) can of tomatoes and green chiles, such as Ro-Tel Original
- ¾ cup heavy cream
- 8 oz. ziti pasta
- ½ tsp. salt
- ½ tsp. pepper
- ½ cup Monterey Jack cheese, shredded
- ½ cup cheddar cheese, shredded

Instructions:
1. Cut sausage into coins. Add olive oil to an oven-safe skillet over medium high heat until shimmering. Add sausage and onions and cook until onions are soft and sausage begins to brown, about 4 minutes. Add garlic and cook an additional 30 seconds.
2. Add broth, tomatoes, cream, ziti, salt and pepper and stir. Bring to a boil, cover skillet, and reduce heat to medium-low. Simmer until pasta is al-dente, about 12 minutes.
3. Mix shredded cheeses together. Remove skillet from heat

and stir in 1/2 cup cheese mixture.
4. Top with remaining cheeses and broil 2 minutes, or until cheese is melted.

***

USA Today bestselling author **Nikki Sloane** landed in graphic design after her careers as a waitress, a screenwriter, and a ballroom dance instructor fell through. Now she writes full-time and lives in Kentucky with her husband, two sons, and a pug who is more slug than dog.

She is a four-time Romance Writers of America RITA© & Vivian Finalist, a Passionate Plume winner, a Goodreads Choice Awards semifinalist, and couldn't be any happier that people enjoy reading her sexy words.

Wings Two Ways
Nina Crespo

One of the things that my husband and I loved about living in National Harbor, Maryland, was having a selection of restaurants in walking distance. Our go-to, Friday-night date spot was the brewery next door. Their craft beer and wings were always the perfect way to end the week.

We're no longer in Maryland, but we still enjoy an early kickoff to the weekend at home with wings and a beverage.

Lemon Pepper Wings (wet)
Yield: 12-14 pieces
Total baking time: 45-50 minutes at 425 degrees

INGREDIENTS
Wings:
2 lbs. whole chicken wings (approximately 6-7 whole wings)
1 cup mojo criollo marinade (store bought or homemade)
¼ cup olive oil
1 clove of chopped garlic
Salt and pepper (optional)

Lemon Pepper Sauce:
1-2 tbsp lemon pepper seasoning (store bought or homemade)
4 tbsp melted butter (or a combination of butter and olive oil)
Juice from ½ medium-sized lemon
1-2 tbsp honey

101

Directions

1. Split each wing into three parts – drumette, wingette, and the tip. Discard the tips.
2. Combine mojo criollo marinade, olive oil, and garlic in a non-metal bowl or shallow dish. Add wings and marinate for at least two hours in the refrigerator. If marinade does not cover the chicken, rotate the wings (drumettes and wingettes) halfway through the marinading time.
3. Preheat oven to 425 degrees. Line a baking sheet with parchment paper or foil and place a wire rack on the baking sheet. Lightly oil the wire rack.
4. Remove chicken from marinade and pat dry with paper towels. Discard the marinade.
5. Place the wings on the rack in a single layer and spread out so they will crisp evenly. Season lightly with salt and pepper, if desired. Place wings on the middle rack of the oven. Flip the wings halfway through the cooking time and continue baking.
6. While the wings are baking, whisk together lemon pepper seasoning, melted butter, lemon juice, and honey.
7. Remove the wings from the oven when done and toss in the lemon pepper sauce. Remove from the sauce and serve.

*Cooking tips:

Wings:
- Dry the wings well before baking. This helps the wings become crispy.
- If the wings start to burn in the oven, decrease the temperature, and increase the cooking time.

Lemon pepper sauce:
- Prepare the sauce with lowest amount of lemon pepper seasoning and honey and increase to taste.
- Substitute part of the lemon juice with mojo criollo.
- Make additional sauce for dipping.

Seasoned Chicken Wings (dry)
Nina Crespo

Yield: 12-14 pieces
Total cooking time: 40-45 minutes

INGREDIENTS
Wings:
2 lbs. whole chicken wings (approximately 6-7 whole wings)
½ tbsp garlic powder
2 tbsp chicken broth base
2 tbsp of favorite dry rub seasoning (Example: Old Bay Seasoning®, barbecue dry rub)
Salt and pepper (optional)

DIRECTIONS
1. Split the wings into three parts – drumette, wingette, and the tip. Throw away the tips.
2. Place your wings (drumettes and wingettes) in a medium- to large-size pot and add enough water to cover the chicken. Add garlic powder and chicken base to the water. Bring water with chicken to a rolling boil. Cover the pot with a lid and decrease temperature from a rolling boil to a low boil/rapid simmer. Cook chicken for 20 minutes.
3. While the chicken is boiling, line a baking sheet with parchment paper or foil and place a wire rack on the baking sheet. Lightly oil the wire rack. Preheat oven to 425 degrees.
4. Once chicken has boiled for 20 minutes, remove wings from the pot and pat dry with paper towels. Place the wings on the rack in a single layer. Spread the wings out so they will crisp

evenly. Baste the wings with butter, season lightly with salt and pepper, if desired, and sprinkle on the dry rub seasoning. Place wings on the middle rack of the oven and bake for 20 minutes or until done, flipping the wings halfway through the baking time.

5. Remove the wings from the oven when they are done baking and serve with your favorite dipping sauce.

*Cooking tips:

Wings:
- If the wings start to burn during baking, decrease the temperature and increase the cooking time.

Seasoning:
- With salty, spicy, or seasonings with a strong flavor, start with less. Once the wings are out of the oven, taste one. If needed, add a bit more seasoning to wings while they are still hot.

***

Nina Crespo is the author of steamy, flirty, sexy reads that satisfy your desire to escape into the wonderful world of "happy for now" or "happily ever after". Wine and coffee often fuel her imagination.

Peanut Butter Chicken Stew
Blake Oliver

This is a great oh-no-I-don't-have-a-dinner-plan meal. Everything can be kept in the pantry or the freezer, which can be thawed in the microwave. Forty minutes, start to finish.

Ingredients:
   1 T. vegetable oil
   1 lb. boneless, skinless chicken breasts, cut into 1-inch pieces
   1 ½ c. chopped onion
   4 garlic cloves, minced
   1 28-oz. can stewed tomatoes
   ½ c. creamy peanut butter
   1 tsp. chili powder
   ½ tsp. salt
   ¼ tsp. crushed red pepper flakes or to taste
   3 c. hot cooked rice or pasta
   ½ c. chopped dry roasted peanuts

Directions:
1. Heat the oil in a large skillet over medium high heat. Add the chicken, onion, and garlic. Cook 5 minutes or until the chicken is brown and onion is tender. Stir in the tomatoes, peanut butter, chili powder, salt, and red pepper flakes.
2. Bring to a boil. Reduce the heat and simmer, covered, for about 30 minutes. Serve over the rice or pasta. Sprinkle with the peanuts.

Makes about 6 servings.

Shrimp-Pistachio Pasta
Blake Oliver

A guy sold me a lamp and gave me this recipe. The recipe has lasted longer than the lamp.

Ingredients:
8 T. (1 stick) butter
1 thumb of ginger, about 2 inches long, peeled and minced
3-4 cloves garlic, minced
2 1-lb. packages frozen shrimp, deveined and tails removed
1 jalapeno, seeded and chopped
Juice of ½ lime
4 green onions, sliced
2/3 to ¾ c. pistachios, shelled and crushed
Angel hair pasta or basmati rice

Directions:
1. Melt butter in large skillet over medium heat.
2. Add ginger and garlic and sauté about 1 minute.
3. Add shrimp, jalapeno, and green onions and sauté an additional 2-3 minutes or until shrimp is pink.
4. Add lime juice. Add pistachios.
5. Serve over angel hair or basmati rice.

***

Blake Oliver writes, wrangles dogs, and fails to resist sweets in an old house on the river in the South.

Dave's Grilled Chicken
A.S. Fenichel

Courtesy of my husband Dave

When I first met my husband, I was widowed, sad, and unsure of myself. Dave was the person who kept telling me that everything was going to be okay. He was a light in the darkness, and very romantic. And he cooks! I love to cook, but it's twice as fun with a partner who also enjoys it. One of the first things he made me was his grilled chicken. Sounds simple right? Everybody makes grilled chicken breasts, but they are often dry and flavorless. This is the best grilled chicken breast you will ever have. Eighteen years later, I love it just as much as the first time. Maybe it tastes so good because it reminds me that Dave was my knight in shining armor when I really needed one. Maybe, it just tastes so darn good!

What you need:
> A pound of boneless chicken breasts. If they're really thick, you might want to butterfly them or adjust cooking time. I'm not a fan of pounded chicken, but you can decide what's best for you.
> ¼ cup soy sauce
> ¼ cup olive oil
> 1 heaping Tbsp garlic powder
> 1 tsp black pepper

About two hours before you're planning to grill, put all ingredients in a plastic storage bag to marinate. Give it a good mush around to combine and make sure the chicken is covered. Put it in the refrigerator and in an hour flip the bag.

To Cook:
1. Heat your grill to medium.
2. Take the chicken out of the marinade and discard the excess.
3. Cook the chicken on the grill for about 4 minutes per side. You can adjust this depending on the thickness of the chicken. I try to keep the breasts about ½ - ¾ thick, and this timing works.

This goes great when sliced over a nice salad, or with rice. It sounds so simple, but the flavors are amazing.

Andie's Spaghetti Sauce with Fresh Pasta
A.S. Fenichel

While both Dave and I cook, in this house there are certain things we each make individually. Some things, like fresh pasta, we make together. It's always a big deal when we make fresh pasta. Not that it's hard, but it is time consuming and very messy. These are good days, and we love to do it.

The sauce, if it's a red sauce, is all me. Other sauces we might make together, or Dave might be the chef, but Marinara is my domain. You wouldn't think a Jewish girl from New Jersey would make great sauce, gravy to those of you from Philly, but mine is the best.

Dave and I spent the first six days of our Italian honeymoon in a cooking school. We loved it and that's where I learned to make a basic marinara. After that, I added my own tweaks to make it really great. It's so good, I often can it and give it as gifts. I love to make a giant pot of sauce and sip some red wine. It's my own kind of Zen. It brings me back to Tuscany and those first days of our married life. Every morning, we cooked with nine other students, then ate the fruits of our labor. Then, in the afternoon, we would visit a vineyard, wine cellar, or walled city. In the evenings, we shared a lovely dinner with our new friends. It was perfect.

For this recipe, we're just making enough to feed some good friends, maybe six. And, just so you know, I use dry pasta all the time. If you're not into making your own, just buy a pound of pasta and follow the directions on the box. However, I highly recommend making your own sauce.

WARNING-You might never go back to a jar sauce again.

109

For the Pasta:

> 2 cups all-purpose flour (You can mix semolina if you like a heavier pasta. If you use only semolina, the dough will be very hard to work with.) Keep the flour out for dusting the board.
>
> 3 large eggs

Some people say you have to do this all by hand, but I always start with an electric mixer. I add the flour and the eggs, then use the dough hook to mix until it forms a ball. Then I flour the board and knead the dough for a good ten minutes until it starts to get elastic. If it gets sticky, add a bit more flower to the board. Put the dough aside with a damp paper towel over it and let it rest for 10-20 minutes.

This next part is best if you have the pasta attachment for your mixer, though it can be done with a manual pasta machine or a rolling pin, if you have that kind of energy.

1. Cut your dough into manageable pieces. Probably six. Keep the dough you're not working with under the moist towel, or it will dry out and become difficult to work with.
2. Flatten the piece you're working with to a thickness of around 1/3 inch using your hand or a rolling pin. You just need it flat enough so the pasta machine can grab it.
3. Now run it through the pasta machine at the largest setting. Fold it in three and do it again. You need to do this TEN times. I'm not kidding...count them.
4. After ten times, the dough will be elastic enough that you can start lowering the settings, one notch at a time to make a nice thin pasta. If 1 is your largest setting, go to 2, run it through, go to three run it through and so on until you get to your desired thickness. I don't recommend you go too far or your pasta will dissolve in the water. I usually go to about 6.
5. I like to hand cut my pasta into Tagliatelle, but you can use whatever tools you like to cut your pasta. Flour the cut pasta, and if you can, lay it flat to dry or hang it on a pasta rack. If you don't have a rack or the space you can make it into little nests as long as you flour it well. It's going to dry out while you get the rest of your dinner ready, but that's perfectly fine.

For the Sauce:
   3 Tbsp olive oil
   1 small onion chopped
   Salt and Pepper to taste.
   2 cloves garlic chopped
   ¼ tsp red pepper flake (optional)
   1 cup red wine (optional)
   2 beef bouillon cubes (highly recommended, but also optional)
   2 - 15 oz. cans of diced tomatoes
   1 - 3oz can of tomato paste
   If you have a parmesan rind that you would normally toss away, put it in the sauce and take it out before serving.
   (If you want to add ground beef or sausage, go for it, just brown it first. Meatballs are also a welcome addition.)

1. Heat olive oil on medium in a large pot with a heavy bottom. I use a Dutch oven, but any sturdy pot will work.
2. Add the onion, salt, and pepper to the oil, then sauté on a medium flame for 5 – 7 minutes, until translucent.
3. Add garlic and sauté for 2 minutes.
4. Add red pepper flake if you like a little heat. Stir frequently for another two minutes.
5. Add red wine and cook until the alcohol is cooked off, about 5 minutes.
6. Now stir in the bouillon cubes, tomatoes, and tomato paste. Let this come to a simmer, then taste. Add more salt if needed.
7. If you have that parmesan rind, go ahead and drop it in now. Just remember to fish it out and toss it before you serve.
8. Lower the heat and let the pot simmer for a minimum of 30 minutes. If I have the time, I let it go for two hours, but a half an hour will still make a great sauce.

To Serve:
1. Boil your fresh pasta for about two minutes, then drain and finish in the sauce. You don't want your pasta to swim in sauce, so removed extra sauce if needed. You can always add it back or serve it on the side like gravy for guests who are *saucy*.

2. If you're using dry pasta, follow the cooking directions on the box, minus one minute, so that you can finish in the sauce and still have al-dente noodles.

***

A.S. Fenichel (Andrea) gave up a successful IT career in New York City to pursue her lifelong dream of being a professional writer. She's never looked back.

Andrea adores writing stories filled with love, passion, desire, magic and maybe a little mayhem tossed in for good measure. Books have always been her perfect escape and she still relishes diving into one and staying up all night to finish a good story.

She is currently writing Regency romance for Kensington Publishing and you can learn more about Andrea's books at http://asfenichel.com or visit her on her Facebook page, where she spends entirely too much time. https://www.facebook.com/A.S.Fenichel.

Originally from New York, she grew up in New Jersey, and now lives in Missouri with her real-life hero, her wonderful husband and a fussy cat. When not reading or writing she enjoys cooking, travel, history, and puttering in her garden.

Ground Beef Stroganoff
Betty Bolté

My beloved mother-in-law shared her recipe for Ground Beef Stroganoff with me when I married her son 30+ years ago. This is my adapted version which I serve to my husband on special occasions because of the associated memories of eating this yummy dish with his parents, both of whom have passed now.

Ingredients
    1.5 lb. lean ground beef
    1 small yellow onion, chopped
    1 clove garlic finely chopped
    1 small can sliced mushrooms, chopped (optional)
    1 can cream of chicken soup
    1 T flour
    8 oz. sour cream
    Minced parsley
    Chow Mein noodles or rice

Directions
1. Brown the ground beef with the onion and garlic.
2. Sprinkle with flour and stir to combine and thicken. Stir in the mushrooms and soup and let simmer for a few minutes. Stir in the sour cream and let it warm through.
3. Serve over noodles or hot rice. Sprinkle with parsley to taste.

Main Dishes

***

Award-winning author **Betty Bolté** is known for authentic and accurately researched historical fiction with heart and supernatural romance novels. A lifetime reader and writer, she's worked as a secretary, freelance word processor, technical writer/editor, and author. She's been published in essays, newspaper articles/columns, magazine articles, and nonfiction books but now enjoys crafting entertaining and informative fiction, especially stories that bring American history to life. She earned a Master's Degree in English in 2008, emphasizing the study of literature and storytelling, and has judged numerous writing contests for both fiction and nonfiction. She lives in northern Alabama with her loving husband of more than 30 years. Her cat, Calliope, serves as her muse and writing partner, and her dog, Zola, makes sure she goes outside frequently. She loves to cook, travel, read, crochet and take long walks.

Grilled Chicken Skewers
RaeAnne Thayne

Our friend is a beekeeper and provides the absolute best locally sourced honey. This makes a delicious, refreshing all-in-one meal on a summer evening. I love that you can really use any combination of vegetables and it always ends up delicious.

Ingredients
¼ cup vegetable oil
⅓ cup honey
⅓ cup soy sauce or liquid aminos substitute
¼ teaspoon ground black pepper
6 skinless, boneless chicken breast halves, cut into 1 inch cubes
2 cloves garlic
2 small onions cut into 2 inch pieces
2-3 red bell peppers, cut into 2 inch pieces
2 yellow squash or zucchini, cut into 2 inch pieces
1 cup mushrooms

Directions
1. In a large bowl, whisk together oil, honey, soy sauce and pepper.
2. Divide in half in zippered bag. Marinate chicken in one bag and vegetables in the other, for at least 2 hours.
3. Preheat the grill for high heat

4. Drain marinade from the chicken and vegetables, reserving marinade from the vegetables.
5. Thread chicken and vegetables alternately onto the skewers.
6. Grill for 12-15 minutes, until chicken juices run clear.
7. Turn and brush with marinade frequently.

***

New York Times, USA Today and #1 Publishers Weekly bestselling author **RaeAnne Thayne** finds inspiration in the beautiful northern Utah mountains where she lives with her family. Her stories have been described as "poignant and sweet," with "beautiful, honest storytelling that goes straight to the heart."

Salmon Patties
Aliza Mann

My mom made these for breakfast (served with piping hot grits), lunch (with a garden salad), or dinner (with rice and a little brown gravy). No matter the meal she chose, they were a crowd pleaser. Being a mom myself now, I now know efficiency was probably another great reason to make them.

Ingredients:
>2 14-ounce cans of wild caught salmon (or pink salmon)
>2 large eggs
>1 bunch of green onions (6 – 8 stalks)
>½ cup of crumbled saltine crackers
>½ lemon – juiced
>1 tablespoon black pepper (or to taste)
>½ teaspoon garlic powder (optional)
>½ cup vegetable oil

Directions:
1. Drain salmon
2. Place in large bowl
3. Pick out bones and skin
4. Add eggs, chopped green onions, saltine cracker crumbs, lemon juice and combine using your hands or a potato masher.
5. Make 8 patties, round and no more than 1 inch thick each.

6. Heat large cast iron skillet over medium high heat.
7. Once the pan is warm, add vegetable oil. Heat until oil sizzles from a drop of water.
8. Cooking in batches based on size of pan (usually four will fit with approx. ½ inch between each), place salmon patties in pan and cook until golden brown on each side. 5 – 10 minutes on each side.

Serve warm or hot.

Recipe Notes:

- Pairs well with fresh salad, rice, grits, or collard greens.
- Cast iron skillet optional, but the heat distribution is perfect for all types of dishes.
- Oil substitutions are okay for this recipe – such as avocado, olive (careful of the low burn point), etc.

(Makes 8 large patties, Serves 4 – 8)

***

Aliza Mann was born in the deep south in a little town called Elberton, GA. Despite living in Michigan now, she still holds the recipes of her ancestors near and dear to her heart. She grew up writing short stories to entertain family and friends and learning to cook beside her mother. Her favorites were sweet breads and included chocolate. Author of paranormal and contemporary romance novels with their strong, quirky heroines in common, she continues to write the love stories of her heart. And perhaps, still eats just a little too much chocolate.

Go Big or Go Home Lasagna
Terri Osburn

I'll preface this by saying there isn't an ounce of Italian heritage in me (I have the DNA results to prove it) but I grew up in a very Italian town and it's my favorite type of food. Many moons ago I had a roommate who made this amazing lasagna, and I convinced her to teach me. I've made my own tweaks to it over the years so here is my simple, sure to please lasagna recipe. I've made this for the holidays but mostly it's good anytime you either have several friends and family to feed, or you just feel like making something yummy that will last for days. This can also be assembled and frozen to pop in the oven a day or two later. Just don't put a frozen glass dish into a hot oven.

Ingredients:
>   3 lbs Ground beef
>   1 lb Italian Sausage
>   3 lbs Shredded Mozzarella Cheese
>   15 oz Ricotta Cheese
>   3 quarts Spaghetti Sauce (I use Prego but your choice just make
>   it somewhat thick)
>   1 box Lasagna noodles

Directions:
1. Preheat the oven to 350 degrees.
2. Put the noodles on to cook. Keep them al dente since they'll continue to cook once the whole thing is in the oven. Brown the ground beef (80/20 or leaner.) Brown the Italian sausage (I use sweet but choose to your taste.) Combine sauce, ground beef, and sausage into a large sauce pan. Set aside until the noodles are done.
3. Once the noodles are cooked, drain and you're ready to assemble. Use a large cake pan or casserole dish the same length as the

noodles and the width of three noodles side by side. You should have your pan, the sauce/meat combo, and your cheeses all spread out.

Assembly:
1. Put a thin layer of sauce mix to cover the bottom of the pan.
2. Lay down three noodles side by side. (1)
3. Cover the noodles with sauce mixture.
4. Sprinkle on a layer of mozzarella (use an Italian combination of cheeses if preferred.)
5. Another layer of noodles. (2)
6. Cover with a layer of sauce mixture.
7. Spread ricotta cheese atop this layer. (I add dollops of cheese since it'll spread out once the next layer goes on.)
8. Sprinkle mozzarella cheese atop the ricotta.
9. Another layer of noodles. (3)
10. Cover with sauce mixture.
11. Sprinkle on a layer of mozzarella
12. One more layer of noodles (4)
13. Cover with sauce mixture. (Should be the last of the sauce.)
14. Sprinkle on mozzarella.
15. Cover with aluminum foil, puncture foil a few times to let the steam out, and bake for 30 minutes.

Makes 9-12 servings depending on serving size.

***

Terri Osburn writes contemporary romance with heart, hope, and lots of humor. After landing on the bestseller lists with her Anchor Island Series, she moved on to the Ardent Springs series, which earned her a Book Buyers Best award in 2016. Terri's work has been translated into five languages, and has sold more than 1.5 million copies worldwide. She resides in middle Tennessee with four frisky felines, and two high-maintenance terrier mixes.

CHEESY CHICKEN
Teri Wilson

This recipe is another yummy sentimental favorite of mine, because a friend brought it to me the day after I came home with my new baby when my son Cameron was born.

Ingredients
    8 chicken thighs
    1 can cream of chicken soup
    1 cup sour cream
    Juice of 1 lemon
    3 tablespoons Worcestershire sauce
    10 ounces sharp cheddar cheese, grated
    3 tablespoons fresh parsley, minced
    ½ cup Ritz crackers, crushed
    3 tablespoons melted butter

Directions
1. Place chicken in 13 x 10 casserole dish.
2. Bake at 350 degrees for 20 minutes.
3. Pour off grease, discard.
4. Combine next 6 ingredients and mix well.
5. Pour over chicken.
6. Combine cracker crumbs and butter.
7. Sprinkle over top.
8. Bake at 400 degrees. Serve over rice.

***

Teri Wilson is a USA TODAY bestselling author of heartwarming, whimsical contemporary romance and Hallmark Channel movies. Lover of crowns, cute dogs and pretty dresses.

Baked Spaghetti
Melanie Greene

A friend brought me this baked spaghetti as I was recovering from surgery once, and I immediately begged her for every detail. It was a huge hit with the whole family, and even better the day after baking. It's easy to double, to freeze, and to modify for most diets.

Ingredients
16 oz. spaghetti noodles
1½ pounds lean ground turkey (or beef, or a vegetarian substitute, etc.)
1 yellow onion, chopped
26 oz. jar of spaghetti sauce (or your own recipe)
15 oz. can tomato sauce
¼ - ½ tsp each oregano and black pepper, to taste
24 oz. container cottage cheese (fat free, low fat, your choice)
1 cup grated mozzarella (I often add closer to 2 cups, because: yum.)

Directions
1. Grease your baking dish (one 9x13 or two square ones.) Preheat oven to 350°.
2. Boil spaghetti noodles according to package directions and drain. Put half the noodles in the bottom of the dish(s), then spread the cottage cheese over the noodles. Cover with the rest of the noodles.
3. Meanwhile, sauté your meat and onion in vegetable oil until the meat is browned, and drain. Blend the meat with the spaghetti and tomato sauces, the oregano, and the pepper. Pour the mixture over the top of the noodles.
4. Cover with foil and bake for one hour. Uncover and top with the grated cheese. Bake 5-10 more minutes to melt the cheese.

***

Melanie Greene lives in a small cottage in a big city and writes contemporary romance featuring lots of laughter and love.

Picnic-Ready Salmon Sandwiches
Catherine Stuart

The original rub recipe comes from my husband, and my mom added the recipe for the garlic spread for an amazing combination. Instead of date nights, my husband and I prefer to go on 'day dates.' These can involve hiking or sitting on a beach on the rocky coast of Maine. These easy-to-make sandwiches pack up well for these outings, and they're a little more romantic than peanut butter and jelly.

Ingredients
>2 sandwich-size salmon fillets
>4 slices of good sandwich bread, such as sliced sour dough or French
>good olive oil
>salt and pepper
>1 cup of arugula

Rub Ingredients
>1 tbsp. paprika
>1 tbsp. brown sugar
>½ tbsp. black pepper
>½ tbsp. salt
>½ tbsp. cumin
>½ tsp. garlic powder
>½ tsp. onion powder
>salt and pepper to taste

Garlic Spread Ingredients
>1 cup plain Greek yogurt
>2 tsps. lemon juice
>1 tsp. minced garlic
>½ tsp. corn starch (optional)
>salt and pepper to taste

Step 1 Preheat the oven to 400 degrees Fahrenheit.

Step 2. Prepare the salmon.
1. Mix rub ingredients into a small bowl, or use a pre-mixed bottle of BBQ rub designed for pork or fish. Pat mixture onto the salmon, forming a crust.

> 2. Lightly spray a cookie sheet with non-stick cooking spray. Place seasoned salmon on the sheet, skin down, making sure not to crowd them.

Step 3. Prepare the sandwich bread.
1. Lightly spray another cookie sheet with non-stick cooking spray.
2. Spread out the bread in one layer on the cookie sheet. You may need an additional cookie sheet to fit all the slices, but some creative placement can let you fit it all on to one sheet.
3. Drizzle a little bit of olive oil across the bread and sprinkle with salt and pepper.

Step 4. Cook the salmon and sandwich bread.
1. Cook salmon in the oven until its internal temperature reaches 145 degrees Fahrenheit, about 10 minutes, depending on how thick the salmon is. For extra-crispy skin, cook salmon on the stove top in a cast iron skillet first, before placing in the oven.
2. At the same time, place your slices of sandwich bread into the oven. With luck, your bread should be golden brown at the same time your salmon is ready to come out. If you have limited oven space, you can simply toast the bread in a toaster, and add seasoning after.

Step 5. Prepare the garlic spread
1. Drain any liquid that has risen to the surface of the yogurt.
2. Whisk together the yogurt, lemon juice, and garlic. Adding in corn starch will help absorb some of the moisture, keeping the spread from being too runny. Add salt and pepper to taste.

Step 6. Assemble the sandwiches
1. Put garlic spread on the unseasoned side of the bread, and assemble with 1 piece of salmon and ½ cup of arugula.

Note: The salmon tastes even better the next day. You can double the recipe and store separate from the bread, or the bread will get quite soggy.

***

Catherine Stuart works as a data geek by day and a novelist by night, spinning tails with quirky heroines and flirty romance. Her first novel was a finalist for the Romance Writers of America's Golden Heart® Award, and she is currently hard at work writing the next three books in the series, following the adventurous of the Beachamp sisters. Catherine lives in coastal Maine with her hot husband, two rambunctious kids, one fluffy dog, and a demonic cat.

Parmesan Chicken
Beth Carter

This mouth-watering chicken dish has been our most-requested family entree for the past forty years! It's exceptional.

Ingredients
    4-6 chicken breasts
    ¾ Cup dry bread crumbs
    1/3 cup grated parmesan cheese
    ¼ cup almonds, sliced or slivered (optional but good!)
    2 T. dried parsley
    1 tsp. salt
    ¼ tsp. pepper
    ¼ tsp. ground thyme
    1 stick butter, melted
    1 tsp. garlic powder

Directions
1. Preheat oven to 350 degrees.
2. Combine crumbs cheese, almonds, parsley, salt, pepper, pepper, and thyme in a mixing bowl.
3. Meanwhile place butter in a 9 x 13 baking dish for 2-3 minutes until butter is melted.
4. Sprinkle with garlic.
5. Dip chicken in butter and then in crumb mixture.
6. Place in the baking dish.
7. Cook uncovered for 45-50 minutes. Do not turn chicken. Cover with foil if it gets too brown toward the end.

Serves: 4-6

Simple Meatloaf
Leslie Hachtel

No one in my family cooked, so if I hadn't learned, I might have starved. Anyway, I improvised this recipe since I love meatloaf and I'm basically a lazy cook. The meat has to be lean or it will be too greasy.

Ingredients
- 1 pound ground sirloin (93%/7%) or 1 pound lean ground turkey
- 1 cup chunky salsa (hot, medium or mild)
- 1/3 cup seasoned bread crumbs (gluten-free or regular)

Directions
1. Preheat the oven to 350 degrees. Line a loaf pan with non-stick tin foil.
2. Put the meat in a bowl with the salsa and mix well. It will be squishy. Add ½ of the bread crumbs and mix. Put meat mixture in a loaf pan and form into a loaf shape. Sprinkle the top with the remaining bread crumbs. Cover with tin foil. Bake at 350 for an hour and remove the tin foil cover. Bake for another 15 minutes. Enjoy.

Serve with mashed potatoes.

Chapter Five
Side Dishes

Family–Hour Spinach Nuggets
Judi Fennell

We call these "Family Hour Spinach Nuggets" because, for years, this was one of the things I brought to our neighborhood "Family Hour" every Friday night from Memorial Day through Labor Day. They'd started out being called "Happy Hours" but when we realized the kids were writing about them in their school summer journals, we decided we needed to change the name *pronto*. Hence... Family Hour.

This would be the perfect thing for mom-of-five, Beth Hamilton, to have on hand as healthy snacks for her kids in *What A Woman Needs*, the second of my Manley Maids series about three brothers who lose a poker bet to their sister who owns a cleaning service, Manley Maids. Satisfaction Guaranteed.

I think you'll be pretty satisfied with these!

Ingredients
   (2) 10-oz pkgs frozen chopped spinach
   1 T dried minced onion
   3 T butter
   1 C Stove Top stuffing mixture
   1 C grated parmesan cheese
   2 eggs, beaten

To make the nuggets
1. Cook spinach and onion together. Drain.
2. Mix hot spinach/onions with butter.

3. When melted, add stuffing mix and parmesan cheese.
4. Stir in eggs.
5. Put in the refrigerator for a half hour.
6. Preheat oven to 375.
7. Then shape spinach mixture into balls with a melon baller.
8. Put on greased baking sheet.
9. Bake for 20 minutes. Makes about 2.5 dozen nuggets.

***

Judi Fennell, #1 Amazon and award-winning author, loves love and loves to laugh, so there's some in every book she writes. Check out her light-hearted, tongue-in-cheek paranormal and romantic comedies at www.JudiFennell.com. From mermen to genies, to men in maid's uniforms and male strippers, there's always a laugh and love to be had. In her spare(?) time, she helps authors with writing and indie-publishing with her formatting, cover/promotional design, editorial, company, www.formatting4U.com. Judi's family includes many four-legged friends, and the minute those creatures start A) singing, B) sewing clothing, or C) cleaning the house will be the day she retires from writing...

Tropical Sweet Potatoes
Gail Chianese

Many years ago, like in another lifetime, I was at a family gathering. It might have been Thanksgiving, and my grandmother served this dish. I always loved sweet potatoes, but I hated "candied yams." They were just too sweet, but this was like a good compromise—just a touch of sweetness and super simple to make. Over the years, this has become a family favorite. I'm not allowed to bring anything else to my in-laws for the holidays, as my sister-in-law is afraid that I won't make this, and it's the only time she gets to enjoy this favorite dish of hers.

Ingredients
2 large sweet potatoes
1 8-oz can crushed pineapple
¼ c. unsweetened coconut
2 T brown sugar
2 T butter

Directions
1. Bake the sweet potatoes, peel, and mash.
2. Then mix in the rest of the ingredients and pop in the oven at 350 degrees for 15-20 minutes or until hot.
3. Serve and enjoy.

***

Gail Chianese is a multi-published author of contemporary romance, romantic mystery, and women's fiction. Originally from California, (she's lived in eight states and three countries thanks to the US Navy) and now calls Connecticut home with her real-life hero of a husband, her three amazing kids and too many animals to count.

Beans for a Crowd
Nikki Brock

Did someone say bacon? This dish is perfect for a potluck; it makes enough to feed an army. Add chunks of ham and you have a great winter night one-pot dish. Bonus: slow cooker!

Did I mention bacon?

Any beans can be substituted for this recipe except the pork and beans. Liquid Smoke usually can be found with the Worcestershire and hot sauce at the grocery. Don't try to substitute. Been there, done that.

Ingredients:
¾ lb. bacon, cut into small pieces
1 c. chopped onion
2 cans pork and beans
1 can kidney beans, drained
1 can butter beans, drained
1 can green beans, drained
1 can garbanzo beans, drained
½ c. brown sugar
1 c. ketchup
1 tsp. salt
½ tsp. pepper
1 T. Liquid Smoke
3 T. white vinegar

Directions:
1. Brown bacon and onions in a skillet; drain off fat. Add bacon and onions to all the beans in a slow cooker. Whisk together brown sugar, ketchup, salt, pepper, Liquid Smoke, and vinegar; add to bean mixture.
2. Stir together well. Cover and cook on low 4-6 hours. Serves 14-16. If using an over, back at 325 degrees for 1 ¾ hours.

Ella's Stove Top Potatoes
Ella Quinn

My paternal grandfather and I are the only cooks in my family, and he passed away over twenty years ago. But he left me cookbooks. Being the type of person who marches to the beat of my own drum, I like to change recipes to suit my needs and make them my own. I do this using two or more recipes, taking what I like and leaving out the rest. This leaves me with my own creation

We like this recipe not only because it's tasty, but it's easy to make on a boat. I usually serve it as a side with lamb, but pork, beef, or bison will work just as well. I don't think I'd have it with chicken, but if you're vegetarian, it would go well with beans.

Ingredients
I have set ingredients for the recipe, but not set amounts. Adjust the amounts to suit your needs.

Large potatoes peeled and sliced thinly. Yukon Gold or any other thin skin potato will do. I use a mandolin or a food processor depending on the amount.

Onions peeled and sliced thinly

Gruyère or Emmentaler cheese or mix the two grated. If you don't like either of those cheeses, you can substitute aged cheddar cheese or goat cheese.

Preparation
1. Heat the butter in a heavy-based frying pan sized to suit the amount you wantthat is about 8in (20cm) in diameter and about 2in (5cm) deep. Remove from the heat and cover the bottom with a layer of the potatoes.
2. Add a layer of onions over the potatoes and another of grated

cheese, seasoning generously as you go. Continue these layers, finishing with a layer of potatoes and a sprinkling of cheese.
3. Cover tightly with tin foil and a lid. Cook over a very low heat for 45 minutes to 1 hour until potatoes on top are just cooked through when pierced with a sharp knife.
4. Serve cut into slices, straight from the pan.

Mouth-watering Macaroni and Cheese
Belle Calhoune

I call this mac n' cheese recipe the golden ticket recipe, because I have struggled for many years to make a fantastic macaroni and cheese. Sadly, every single time I tried to make it, the macaroni came out overcooked or bland or blah. It just wasn't gooey or creamy or cheesy.

Enter one of the miracles of my life. The slow cooker. Now cue the halo music. Ta Dah! About ten years ago I purchased a slow cooker and began experimenting with recipes. Ribs. Pulled pork. Chicken. Chili. And yes... mac n' cheese. Where had this slow cooker been all my life? As a writer with deadlines, the simplicity of the slow cooker is extremely appealing. This macaroni and cheese recipe is my all-time favorite. I've served it at Thanksgiving, Christmas and upon request from my children. It's that good! And it's very simple to make. And like Charlie in Willie Wonka, I found my golden ticket.

Ingredients
cooking spray
One box of elbow macaroni (cooked and drained)
½ cup of sour cream
1 cup of milk
1 can of condensed cheddar cheese soup any variety
1 ½ cups of (orange) cheddar cheese, 1 1/2 cups of white sharp cheddar cheese, grated
2 eggs
1 teaspoon of Dijon mustard
1 teaspoon of adobo or seasoned salt
½ tsp pepper
3 tablespoons of butter

Directions

1. Lightly spray sides of crock pot. Boil pasta for six minutes, then drain. The crock pot should be set to high. Add pasta to crock pot along with grated cheeses, cheddar soup, sour cream, butter, milk and eggs. Mix all together then add all the seasonings. If desired, add additional cheese or sour cream. You can periodically check back to make sure it is not browning too much at the sides. You can stir every now and again.

2. 2 hours to 2.5 hours on high is pretty near perfection although slow cooker times vary. I often check on it and turn the temp down midway. You can always check on it and look at the sides. If they are browning too much you can always turn the temp down to low. The cheese is very flexible also. You can use different types of cheese or add more or less depending on your taste. Bacon bits can be added to the mac n cheese. Add some lobster for a nice seafood lobster mac n' cheese. Bread crumbs can be sprinkled over the top at the end. Or if you want to add some veggies, broccoli can be placed on top as well.

***

Belle Calhoune grew up in a small town in Massachusetts as one of five children. Growing up across the street from a public library was a huge influence on her life. Married to her college sweetheart and mother to two daughters, she lives in Connecticut. A dog lover, she has a mini poodle and a black lab. She is a Publisher's Weekly Best-selling author as well as a member of RWA's Honor Roll. In 2019 her book "An Alaskan Christmas" was made into a movie (Love, Alaska) by Brain Power Studios and aired on UPTV. She is the author of over 40 novels and published by Harlequin Love Inspired and Grand Central Publishing.

Pecan-Raising Turkey Stuffing
Kat Martin

Christmas is my favorite holiday. To me that means a big family gathering, cooking all day, and sitting down to a table filled with relatives and friends. It always includes a big turkey stuffed with old-fashioned dressing, giblet gravy, mashed potatoes and candied yams, fresh vegetables, hot dinner rolls, and pumpkin or pecan pie for dessert.

A dear friend gave me this recipe so long ago I've started claiming it as my own, but every year when I make it, I read the recipe card she gave me. I see her handwriting in fading blue ink, think of the friend I haven't seen in years and feel the faint sting of nostalgic tears. I appreciate her friendship all over again and hope she remembers me as fondly as I remember her.

Ingredients

Turkey neck and giblets cooked in a pot of boiling water until done (about 1½ hours. (Remove and save broth)
1 can chicken broth
2 cubes butter
1 can sliced water chestnuts and juice
1 small can sliced mushrooms and juice
1 small can of olives (drained)
I whole apple chopped (peeling off or on)
I medium onion chopped
½ cup of pecans
¾ cup of raisins
1 egg (optional)
1 box stuffing mix (cornbread or regular)

Directions

1. Peel cooked turkey meat off neck and set aside, saving broth for later. Chop remaining cooked giblets and set aside. (Leave some for turkey gravy.) Pour can of chicken broth into large saucepan. Add sticks of butter. Bring to a low simmer. Add turkey meat. Add mushrooms and juice, water chestnuts, sliced olives, chopped onion, chopped apple, raisins, and pecans. Beat egg and add to mixture. Simmer until onion and apple are cooked.

2. In large missing bowl, place both packets of stuffing mix (I usually buy 2 boxes so I can add a little extra if needed to achieve the right consistency). Pour chicken broth/giblet mixture over stuffing a little at a time, stirring as you go, to get right texture. Add thyme, sage, salt and pepper to taste.

3. When you are finished, stuff your turkey, or grease 9 x 13 inch backing pan, load stuffing into pan, and bake for forty-five minutes at 350 degrees.

4. When you take it out, you will have a great, old-fashioned raisin-pecan stuffing perfect for Thanksgiving or Christmas that I hope will become a family favorite.

***

Currently living outside Missoula, Montana, **Kat Martin** is the New York Times bestselling author of over seventy-five Historical and Contemporary Romantic Suspense novels. Before she started writing, Kat was a real estate broker. During that time, she met her husband, L. J. Martin, an author of Westerns and high-action Thrillers. Kat is a graduate of the University of California at Santa Barbara where she majored in Anthropology and also studied History. She spends her winters in Arizona.

"I love to travel and especially like visiting the places where my books are set," Kat says. "I love history and enjoy spending time in museums and art galleries. My husband and I often stay in out-of-the-way inns and historical houses. It's fun and it gives a wonderful sense of a by-gone era."

To date, Kat has over seventeen million copies of her books in print. She is published in more than two dozen foreign countries, including Germany, France, Norway, Sweden, China, Korea, Bulgaria, Russia, England, South Africa, Italy, Spain, Argentina, Japan and Greece.

Kat is currently writing her next Romantic thriller.

Sweet & Crunchy Brussels Sprouts
Jennifer Bray-Weber

When I was young, my mother tried to get me interested in cooking (and sewing). She had many delicious family recipes to pass down. Plus, she would add, it was a skill I needed for when I left home and had my own family. Yeah, nah. I was content eating what she made, not participating in the actual work. As a teen in the 80s, cooking (and sewing) held no interest to me. I was too busy riding horses bareback, hand-writing lyrics to the latest rock album, and chasing boys. To this day, cooking just isn't my thing (and sewing... forget about it). I'm the type that will balk at whipping up a dish with more than 6 ingredients. Quick and simple is the way I roll. So when I find something stupid easy to make with few ingredients but loads of flavor, I'm all in. That's why I love this fresh and healthy side dish. It's perfect for any occasion or season. Bonus, it's a hit with my family, too. Who knows, maybe this recipe will be passed down to my kids.

Ingredients:
    1 lb. Brussels sprouts
    2 tbsp. olive oil
    1/2 tsp. ground nutmeg
    1/2 c. walnuts
    1/2 c. dried cranberries
    salt
    black pepper

Directions:
1. Shred or slice Brussels sprouts thinly
2. Warm olive oil in skillet over medium heat
3. Add Brussels sprouts, nutmeg, and salt & pepper to taste
4. Cook, stirring until sprouts are bright and wilted (usually just a handful of minutes)
5. Place in serving bowl
6. Toss in cranberries and walnuts

Enjoy

***

Jennifer Bray-Weber is a Texas-born, Texas-bred girl. That means she's loud, proud, and a bit on the sassy side. Okay, really, she tips the scales on the sass. Award-winning and multi-published, Jenn writes historical romances, including the *Romancing the Pirate* series. She also writes steamy paranormal adventures and dabbles in erotic tales as Harlowe Wilde.

She is a married domestic goddess/beach bum with two girls, two dogs, and three felines. She loves the ocean, horses, muscle cars, tattoos, rockin' music, outdoor activities, reading, writing, scrapbooking, traveling, researching, fishing, shopping, dares, the Oxford comma, and, of course, carousing about like a pirate. Her countless questionable, often hilarious, life experiences that can only be told over a few stiff drinks.

English Roast Potatoes
Catherine Hope

1. Preheat oven to 375
2. Peel & quarter potatoes – as many as you'd like
3. Put in pan with well salted water and boil until fork tender
4. Pour out water – reserve for gravy if desired
5. Put pot back on stove, element off, and shake pan to dry off the potatoes until they look rough on the outside but careful they don't fall apart
6. Cover liberally with oil, salt, pepper and if desire onion and/or garlic powder – toss to coat well
7. Turn potatoes into a roasting pan and add oil as needed to cover and leave a coating on the bottom of the pan
8. Place in oven. Don't' try to turn them until they are getting golden, turning too soon will break them. I use a rounded knife to flip them over by scraping under the potato. The more they cook the less they stick. Add more oil if needed.

If you are cooking a roast, potatoes can be put around the roast. I will do this and then when roast is out, move potatoes to another pan with oil and turn heat up on oven and continue to roast until well golden and crunchy

They are done when well browned and crunchy. Tilt the pan so oil drains to one side and off potatoes.

Yorkshire Pudding
Catherine Hope

Prepare earlier in the day and then keep batter in fridge until ready to use.
Equal parts. I use 6 eggs and it makes a nice size pudding:

Ingredients
Flour
Eggs
Milk
Tsp salt (sometimes I add onion or garlic powder for a change)

Directions
1. Combines wet ingredients and add to the flour and mix well. Put in fridge.
2. Preheat oven to 450
3. 9x13 baking pan cover bottom with oil about ¼ inch.
4. Put in oven until hot, almost smoking
5. Remove pudding from fridge and stir it up and had to the hot pan.
6. Put back in oven for about 20 -30 minutes until puffed up.
       ***don't open oven to peek, it will ruin the rise
7. When done it should be a puffed and delicious. Cut to desire portions. May stick to the bottom of the pan and use a sharp edge to loosen.

Herbed Carrots and Zucchini
Roni Denholtz

Ingredients
2 small zucchini, cut into fourths, then crosswise into chunks
1½ cup sliced carrots (approx. 3 medium carrots)
1 onion, cut into small slices (optional)
2 Tbl. water
½ tsp. salt
¼ tsp. pepper if desired
¼ tsp. dried dill or 2/3 tsp. fresh dill

Directions
1. Place all ingredients except zucchini in casserole.
2. Cover tightly and microwave on high for 4 minutes.
3. Add zucchini, and microwave 3-5 minutes more.

This recipe can be doubled or tripled for a crowd, but add 2-3 more minutes of cooking time.

***

Roni Denholtz is an award-winning author of 22 romance novels and novellas, 9 children's books, and over 100 articles and short stories. She lives in beautiful northwest NJ with her husband and adopted dog. She has volunteered for school organizations, her local animal shelter, and is a past president of NJ Romance Writers. Her children are grown and married and she is now a proud grandmother!

Cowboy Beans
Deb Kastner

Summer days are made for grilling hot dogs and hamburgers, and out here in Colorado, Cowboy Beans are one of our favorite side dishes. Great with potato salad!

Ingredients
2 cans pork & beans
2 Tbs brown sugar
½ chopped onion
2 Tbs ketchup
2 Tbs Worcestershire sauce

Directions
1. Mix together in a large baking dish.
2. Bake for 30 minutes at 350 degrees.

***

Publisher's Weekly Bestselling, award-winning author of over 50 novels and two million books in print, **Deb Kastner** writes contemporary sweet and inspirational western romances. Deb lives in beautiful Colorado with her husband, two adorable dogs, two mischievous cats and during her midlife crisis adopted a horse named Moscato. She is blessed with three adult daughters and two grandchildren. Her favorite hobby is spoiling her grandchildren, but she also enjoys traveling, music (The Texas Tenors and The High Kings are her favs), singing in the church choir, and exploring the Rocky Mountains on horseback.

Thanksgiving Sauerkraut with Pork, Apples, and Onions

Mary Jo Putney

I grew up in rural Western New York, then lived in California and England before coming to rest in Baltimore, Maryland. As my first Maryland Thanksgiving approached, a friend mentioned the usual side dishes that accompanied her turkey: squash, dressing, mashed potatoes, cranberry orange relish, sauerkraut...

Whoa, *sauerkraut?!!* I'd never liked sauerkraut and certainly never considered it an essential part of a Thanksgiving dinner, but sure enough, it's A Thing in Baltimore, probably because the city was settled by many German and Eastern European immigrants. So the next year, I dutifully decided to make a batch of sauerkraut. I found the original of this recipe in a crock pot cookbook and made a number of modification.

Much to my surprise, the result was delicious. Long, slow cooking eliminates the sourness and all the ingredients meld together beautifully. My husband, a native Baltimorean with Lithuanian ancestry, loves it. Of course it can be made at any time of the year, but I generally make a very large batch for Thanksgiving, then freeze in smaller quantities to be produced with a flourish through winter. I serve it with mashed potatoes and applesauce.

This is peasant food, so quantities are approximate.

Ingredients

Four pounds or so of fresh sauerkraut, drained.
About 1½ - 2½ pounds of pork chops
Two medium to large onions, sliced
Two apples, cored and sliced (don't need to be peeled. A crisp apple like Granny Smith is best.)
A tablespoon or two of caraway seeds
Half a cup of water with maybe a little salt dissolved in it

145

Directions

1. Trim fat and brown the chops on both sides, seasoning with salt and pepper to taste. Then cut the chops into pieces. The size depends on whether you like large chunks of pork or small ones. The cutting up is easier if you get the expensive boneless pork chops, but any will do.
2. Using a standard size crock pot (slow cooker), layer the ingredients: sauerkraut, pork, apples, and onions, starting and ending with sauerkraut and scattering the caraway seeds as you go.
3. Add the water, cover, and cook in the crock pot on low for six to eight hours. (Pork should be tender and falling apart.) Slow cooking on stove top or in the oven would probably work, but would require more watching.
4. Great with mashed potatoes and maybe applesauce on the side.
5. You'll note that I love freezing food. When I'm on deadline, it's great to pull quarts of soup or sauerkraut or other foods from my freezer so I don't actually have to cook!

***

A *New York Times* bestselling author, **Mary Jo Putney** was born in upstate New York with a reading addiction, a condition with no known cure. Her entire writing career is an accidental byproduct of buying a computer for other purposes. Most of her books contain history, romance, and cats, though she has also written contemporary romance, fantasy, and Young Adult historical fantasy. She has had eleven RWA RITA nominations, two RITA wins, RWA's 2013 Nora Roberts Lifetime Achievement Award, and she's so distractable that she's amazed that she ever finishes a book.

Oyster Crackers in Savory Herbs
Susan Wiggs

The Oysterville Sewing Circle has become a reader favorite, probably because its strong themes of female empowerment and women supporting women is something we can all relate to. This book is best enjoyed with snacks and discussed in the company of friends. It isn't a foodie book, but there's food in the title (unless you're vegan. Sorry, oysters!).

What to eat with my book:
Well, oysters, obviously, but since oysters are controversial ("He was a bold man that first ate an oyster" –Jonathan Swift) and tricky to prepare, there are other options. Instead, let's do oyster CRACKERS. These Ranch Dill Oyster Crackers are vegan-friendly *and* curiously addictive:

Ingredients
> 1 (1 ounce) package Ranch-style dressing mix
> ½ teaspoon dried dill weed
> ¼ cup vegetable oil
> ½ teaspoon lemon pepper (optional)
> ¼ teaspoon garlic powder (optional)
> 5 cups oyster crackers

Directions
1. Preheat oven to 300 degrees F (120 degrees C).
2. In a large bowl, combine the dressing mix, dill weed, vegetable oil, lemon pepper, and garlic powder.
3. Add oyster crackers, and toss to coat. Spread evenly on parchment-lined baking sheets.
4. Bake for 10 minutes, give everything a stir, then bake another 10 minutes. Cool before serving.

Enjoy at your next book club discussion!

And here's a game to play with your book club. Name five fictional characters you'd like to invited to dinner.

My dream dinner table:

I'd love to invite five fictional women to my Oysterville meal, which takes place in Oysterville, Washington. In the novel it's described as "a town perched at the farthest corner of
Washington state. The tiny hamlet hung at the very tip of a narrow peninsula, crooked like a beckoning finger between the placid bay and the raging Pacific."
Around the table, we have Madame Bovary and Juliet Capulet, whom we'll convince to make better choices. Let's also add Margaret Dashwood from SENSE AND SENSIBILITY, because she will be the one to convince them! Another guest—Catniss Everdeen from THE HUNGER GAMES, who will give us lessons in self-defense and survival. And finally, Eleanor Oliphant, because she's so lovable and vulnerable, and we will show her the kindness she deserves.

Who will show up at your table, readers?

***

Susan Wiggs likes to believe she is the person her dogs think she is.
She phones her parents every day, as they are elderly and adorable, and they read her stories every day of her freakishly normal childhood. She was a writer before she learned to read, by creating scribbles on paper and dictating the stories to her saintly mother.
Untold eons later, she still reads and writes every day and she's gotten very good at it. She lives in a ridiculously gorgeous place in the world—an island in Puget Sound, Washington where they have a lot of the same flowers grown in the UK. But bigger slugs. Much bigger slugs.

Macaroni and Cheese
Betty Bolté

A while ago I came across my adored Great-Aunt Julia's recipe for macaroni and cheese and decided to try it. She always made such wonderful meals for us when we'd visit her on the Eastern Shore of Maryland so I thought it would be fun to bring her memory into my home. It took several tries, but now I have a recipe for homemade comfort food I like to make on chilly evenings.

Ingredients
8 oz. macaroni
2 T butter cut into pieces
1½ cups shredded cheese (I like a mix of cheddar and parmesan)
2 eggs, beaten
2 cups milk
Black pepper
Paprika

Directions
1. Heat oven to 350°F.
2. Cook macaroni according to the package directions. Drain.
3. Combine hot macaroni, butter, and cheese in the same pot you cooked the macaroni in. Place the mixture in a 1½ quart baking dish.
4. Combine eggs, milk, and pepper to taste. Pour over macaroni mixture. Sprinkle with paprika.
5. Bake 40-50 minutes.

Potato Salad
Betty Bolté

This is my beloved father's recipe. I love to fix this in the summer time when we're going to be grilling ribs or burgers.

Ingredients
>   6 large russet potatoes
>   3 eggs, hard boiled and peeled
>   1 small yellow onion, chopped
>   2 stalks celery, chopped
>   1 T sweet pickle relish
>   Dill weed, to taste
>   Mayonnaise, to taste
>   Paprika for garnish

Directions
1. Cover potatoes in a large pot with water; boil until fork tender (firm but not soft). Cool on a wire rack.
2. When cool enough to handle, peel potatoes (I use a sharp knife) and cut into bite size pieces and place in a large mixing bowl.
3. Dice one hard-boiled egg and add to potatoes.
4. Add onion, celery, relish, and dill weed to the potatoes, stirring well. Add mayo until desired consistency.
5. Transfer potato salad to serving dish.
6. Slice remaining 2 eggs and lay on top of the potato salad. Sprinkle with paprika.

Note: Let the potato salad chill for several hours or overnight to meld the flavors.

***

Betty Bolté is known for American historical fiction with heart and haunting, bewitching love stories. She has published more than 25 books of fiction and nonfiction.

Grandma Willie's Cornbread Dressing
Leslie Scott

Every time I make this classic southern side dish, I'm reminded fondly of both my grandmother and that first Thanksgiving with Mr. Scott.

Here in the southern United States, holiday gatherings that surround food are a huge deal. Throw a cookout with burgers and hotdogs? We raise you a smoker and our Papaw's secret butt rub and Mama's special banana pudding. Which brings me to one of the Scott family's favorite holiday stories–New England Thanksgiving.

My favorite stepmom, I've had a few, was born and raised in New England. Her father was a council man and alderman, her mother an elementary school principal, and her sister a teacher. How in the world they all ended up in northern Alabama is a mystery to me. But they did and she married my father and that brings us to my and Mr. Scott's first holiday season as a couple.

Mr. Scott has a simple palette and over the years I've managed to expand his tastes (he eats Indian food now, curry and all, which is a miracle). But fifteen years ago, Thanksgiving, we weren't there yet.

At my aunt's home for lunch, we were treated to a spread of traditional southern holiday food (remarkably similar to most of America, I'd imagine). Various casseroles, turkey and ham, deviled eggs, rolls, and all the goodness including my Grandma Willie's cornbread dressing. Of which, Mr. Scott was a big fan.

He sat at the table with my dad, Grandma Willie and several other family members and contemplated a second helping of the dressing but decides against it since we were going to my stepmom's house for dinner that evening. My dad responds that he should get the dressing with an ominous, "you'll need it."

Mr. Scott is from a tiny, tiny town, on top of a mountain, in north-west Alabama. He likes beans, potatoes, and basic meats. Doesn't take much to please him food wise... just no onions, nothing green, and nothing weird looking. He was ill prepared for what my very southern father had termed "New England Thanksgiving."

When we arrived that night, Cliff was treated to a glass of wine and ushered to a table full of appetizers. After munching on a piece of cheese, he points to a dish. "What's that brain looking stuff?"

My dad responds. "That's goose liver pate."

Mr. Scott steered clear of the snacks and waited on the main course. Now, Thanksgiving stuffing isn't called stuffing down here. We have a dressing, and it's cooked on as a side dish and never stuffed inside a bird. I watched his horror-stricken face as a spoon was stuck inside the turkey and stuffing shoveled out. Stuffing made with big chunks of bread, various vegetables, and mushrooms.

Here's where I stop you. The stuffing was lovely, layered with various flavors. But for Mr. Scott, he was out the moment he saw mushrooms.

Next on his plate was green peas, another food he doesn't eat. Considering they are the least offensive vegetable ever; this choice confuses me. But by this point he was getting a little desperate and clinging to the flute of champagne.

By the next dish, he was hopeful. Small potatoes, stewed in a cream sauce. Or so his poor southern heart thought, right up until his first relieved bite.

I'd never until that moment seen someone's face turn multiple shades of green. But there is one vegetable that Mr. Scott cannot eat, that we cut up so small he can't feel them in any food we cool–onions. My stepmom had prepared pearl onions in a cream sauce.

Mr. Scott had no idea such a thing existed.

Mr. Scott was several breaths away from spitting it across the table. He did the one thing he could do and chugged two flutes of champagne (mine and his) to get the taste from his mouth. He shuffled food around on his plate and ate a few tentative bites of turkey. In the car as we were leaving, he rifled through the cooler full of leftovers from my aunt's house earlier in the day.

He ate a plate full of Grandma Willie's dressing on the way home. I still make it today but will occasionally threaten him with pearled onions and stuffed stuffing. I get away with it though, because I know how to make my grandmother's dressing.

Ingredients
- 1 cooked, deboned, and shredded chicken (or rotisserie chicken)
- 1 pan cornbread (follow directions on the back of the cornmeal mix or make your own)
- 1 sleeve saltine crackers
- 1 to 2 yellow onions, finally chopped
- 1 cup chopped celery (optional, I don't usually use it)
- 1 to 2 boxes chicken broth
- 2 eggs
- 1 tablespoon plus (to taste) sage
- 2 teaspoons garlic powder
- 2 teaspoons onion powder
- 2 teaspoons chicken seasoning
- 2 teaspoons poultry seasoning
- Salt and White Pepper to taste

Directions
1. Preheat oven to 375 Degrees Fahrenheit and spray large casserole dish with cooking spray.
2. Crush crackers and crumble cornbread. Add chicken and all dry ingredients to a large bowl and combine thoroughly. Add eggs and one box broth and mix. If dressing is not a thick, soupy consistency add more broth from other box.
3. Poor into prepared casserole dish and bake for 45 minutes or until top is golden brown.
4. Grandma Willie would crumble her finished dressing so that it looked more like stuffing. I've met people who scoop it out in balls with an ice-cream scoop. We just spoon it on onto the plate, put turkey on top of it, and smother them both in gravy.

***

Award winning author of Two Hearts, One Stone and the Arkadia Fast Series, **Leslie Scott** has been writing stories for as long as she can remember. The happier the ending, the better. Currently, she lives and writes amidst her own happily ever after with her soul mate, son, and domestic zoo.

Cornbread dressing
Mindy Neff

Since holidays at our house are large and noisy-I usually cook for a minimum of 30 people-I will often double or triple this recipe and bake it in an aluminum throwaway lasagna or roasting pan. It's my absolute favorite side dish to go with the turkey!

Ingredients
- --2 cups of cornbread
- --½ loaf (6 or 7 slices) of bread
- --1-2 bunches green onions
- --1 bunch celery
- --3 eggs
- --Poultry seasoning to taste (start with 1 or 2 TBS. Add more to your liking)
- --Juice from your turkey giblets (or just use chicken broth)

Directions
1. Finely crumble the cornbread.
2. Sauté onions and celery in butter until translucent.
3. Add eggs, cooked onions and celery, chicken broth and poultry seasoning to the crumbled cornbread. You want this mixture to be slightly soupy, so add more chicken broth as needed.
4. Pour into a 9 x 13 pan and bake at 350 degrees for 45 minutes.

Pasta Salad
Valerie Clarizio

This recipe came from my mother-in-law. It is a family picnic favorite and the most requested side dish for a potluck among my friends.

Ingredients
- 1 LB Thick Pasta
- 1½ C Olive Oil
- 1½ C Vinegar
- 1½ C Sugar
- 1 Tbsp Parsley
- 1½ tsp Pepper
- 1 tsp Salt
- 2 Small Cucumbers
- 1 C Black Olives
- 1 Red Onion
- 1 Green Pepper

Directions
1. Mix the oil, vinegar, and sugar thoroughly.
2. Blend in the parsley, pepper, and salt.
3. Add all other ingredients.

***

Valerie Clarizio is a USA Today bestselling author who lives in romantic Door County Wisconsin with her husband and extremely spoiled cat. She loves to read, write, and spend time at her cabin in the Upper Peninsula of Michigan.

She's lived her life surrounded by men, three brothers, a husband, and a male Siamese cat who required his own instruction manual. Keeping up with all the men in her life has turned her into an outdoors enthusiast, of which her favorite activity is hiking in national parks. While out on the trails, she has plenty of time to conjure up irresistible characters and unique storylines for her next romantic suspense or sweet contemporary romance novel.

Judie's Sweet Noodle Kugel
Meredith Bond

Many Jewish families have their own sweet noodle kugel recipe. My mother made one every Rosh Hashanah, reluctantly, for my father. Her family was from Romania and had savory onion potato kugel which she would make for herself (because the rest of our family preferred the sweet one). Unfortunately, my mother was a lousy cook – the result of having grown up with a mother who was a fantastic cook and wouldn't let anyone into the kitchen when she was at work. Between my grandmother's refusal to teach her, and my mother's complete lack of interest in learning, we were lucky we had something to eat every night for dinner.

Happily, when my father remarried after my mother's death, he married a great cook. I wasn't going to waste such an opportunity, and asked my new step-mother for her kugel recipe. This has now become a staple in my cooking repertoire. I'm sure after you taste it, it will become one in yours as well. It is *so* good!

Ingredients:

12 oz wide egg noodles (remember if you're making this for Passover, they've got to be special, kosher for Passover noodles)

3 eggs

¾ cup sugar

6 oz softened cream cheese

1 ⅛ cup sour cream

1 tsp vanilla

¼ cup raisins

Cinnamon for sprinkling.

Directions:

1. Cook noodles according to package directions.
2. Beat eggs and sugar together in a small bowl and put aside.
3. In a large bowl mix together the rest of the ingredients with the hot, cooked noodles (helps to melt the cream cheese).
4. Add the egg/sugar mixture and mix thoroughly.
5. Pour into a well greased 9x12 baking pan and sprinkle with cinnamon.
6. Bake 1 hour at 350. The top should be a little crisp and slightly browned.

***

Meredith Bond's books straddle that beautiful line between historical romance and fantasy. An award-winning author, she writes fun traditional Regency romances, medieval Arthurian romances, and Regency romances with a touch of magic. Known for her characters "who slip readily into one's heart," Meredith loves to take her readers on a journey they won't soon forget.

Marillen or Zwetschgen Knödel
(apricot or plum dumplings)
Penelope Janu

This recipe was given to me by my beloved mother-in-law, who was Austrian but lived in Australia for many years. She was a wonderful cook, and often said, 'If there is fruit, it is healthy.' The ingredients are basic- but combined they make a delicious dumpling!

Ingredients:
Apricots or plums (fresh fruit including stones – medium sized) – 10
Potatoes (thin skinned, washed) – 5 medium
Plain flour – approximately 1cup
Egg – 1
Butter – approximately 50g (3½ tbs)
Breadcrumbs – 7 heaped tbs
Brown sugar – approximately 10 tsp

Process:
1. Steam potatoes until they have softened (but are still firm). Remove the skin and finely grate. Add a similar volume of flour to the potatoes, add the egg and knead to form a pliable dough.
2. Cover the apricots or plums in the dough and boil them in a large pot of water. Immediately the knödel rise to the surface, remove and place them in a strainer.

159

3. Use a non-stick frying pan to brown the breadcrumbs (in a small amount of butter). When all the knödel are cooked, roll them in the breadcrumbs.
4. Serve with brown sugar.

***

Penelope Janu lives by the coast near Sydney, Australia, with six grown children (who come and go) and a distracting husband. An award winning and much-loved author, she writes contemporary romances about clever and adventurous women who don't mean to fall in love–but do.

Chapter Six
Soups

One Pan Chicken and Dumplings Soup
Cathy McDavid

Perfect for eating with a spoon straight from the pan

Yeah, baby. Comfort food. What can be better? Well, a comfort food dish that's really simple to cook and pretty complete meal all on its own. Daughters who don't eat meat can pick out the chicken. All this dish needs is some dessert. Try it during the holidays with leftover turkey. Yum. In a real hurry? You guessed it. Just spoon straight from the pot, you don't have to bother moving the pot over to the sink. But I might make an exception with this perfect comfort food dish and get cozy with hubby in front of the TV for a Friday night movie marathon, each of us slurping a bowl of this soup.

Ingredients:
   4 cups chicken broth
   1 10.75 oz cream of chicken soup
   2 13-oz cans cooked and shredded chicken (or our own fully
      cooked chicken equal to this amount)
   1 8.75 oz can of corn (can use frozen or fresh cooked corn equal
      to this amount)
   1 4.5 oz can of carrots (again, can use frozen or fresh cooked
      carrots equal to this amount – I prefer fresh cooked carrots
      myself)
   2 16.3 oz tubes of refrigerator biscuits
   Preferred seasonings

Optional: add other cooked vegetables of choice, such as peas, mushrooms, or diced red peppers

163

Preparation:

1. Cut biscuits into quarters and set aside.
2. In a large pot on the stove, heat broth, soup, and chicken until boiling.
3. Cover and reduce to simmer for five minutes.
4. Add the cooked vegetables and biscuit quarters.
5. Cover and simmer for another 20 minutes, stirring frequently to prevent the biscuits from sticking together.

***

Cathy McDavid has been penning Westerns for Harlequin since 2005. With over 50 titles in print and 1.5 million-plus books sold, Cathy is also a member of the prestigious Romance Writers of America's Honor Roll. This "almost" Arizona native and mother of grown twins is married to her own real-life sweetheart. After leaving the corporate world seven years ago, she now spends her days penning stories about good looking cowboys riding the range, busting broncs, and sweeping gals off their feet – oops, no. Make that winning the hearts of feisty, independent women who give the cowboys a run for their money. It a tough job, but she's willing to make the sacrifice,

A self-proclaimed foodie, you'd think she'd be a good cook or, at least, like to cook. Nope on both counts. She dreads hearing the words, "What's for dinner?" Simple, fast, and easy recipes are her go-to secret weapon, and if they're all-in-one meals, so much the better.

Trophy Chili
Heather Heyford

Like many cooks, my 'joy in cooking' comes from developing my own twist on the classics. My mom's chili recipe is a perfect example. Over the years I made dozens of variations in my attempt to make it mine. Until the time I tweaked it by using a sweeter tomato sauce and a can of sweet corn (including the juice) to take to our neighborhood chili cook-off–and came home proudly bearing a first-place trophy. Since then, I haven't changed a thing. Why mess with perfection? Notes: utilize the recommended brands to come as close as possible to the same, prize-worthy results. And–as with many soups and stews–it tastes even better the next day, after the flavors have melded.

In a large stock pot, combine:
> 1 lb. ground beef
> 1 medium onion, chopped
> 2 cloves garlic, minced
> 2 large stalks celery, chopped

Cook, stirring occasionally, on medium heat until meat is browned and onion is soft. If using very low fat beef, you may have to add some oil to prevent sticking. If using higher fat beef, drain before moving on.

Add to pot:
> 40 oz. can kidney beans, drained and rinsed in a colander
> 1 can Green Giant Extra Sweet Niblets corn and juice

3-24 oz. jars Francesco Rinaldi Sweet & Tasty tomato sauce. If unavailable substitute same quantity Ragu original sauce plus 2 tsp. sugar or to taste

2-15 oz. cans plain, stewed or chopped tomatoes and juice

2 tsp. Worcestershire sauce

4 T. chili powder or to taste

3 tsp. salt or to taste

Cook on low, stirring occasionally, tasting for salt, chili powder and sugar. If desired top with shredded cheddar cheese.

***

Heather Heyford's contemporary romance novels are set in the wine country, where she visits frequently to sample pinot noir–er, research her works in progress. She's currently putting the finishing touches on a mainstream novel about three generations of hard-headed, soft-hearted women struggling to navigate our tumultuous times with humor and grace.

Sausage Soup
Mary Jo Putney

I love making soup as much as I love eating it--I have dozens and dozens of recipes. I owe this particular soup, one of my very favorites, to an online discussion of Novelists, Inc., which is a group for writers of popular fiction genres such as romance and mystery. Now and then we go off the rails and stop discussing publishing and start talking food. This recipe is my variation of one invented by author Anne Holmberg. It's easy to make and a hearty full-meal soup.

Ingredients
> 3 lb. bulk sausage, browned over medium heat. (Perhaps one pound hot, other two pounds regular.)
>
> 3- 4 large onions, chopped and fried with the sausage.
>
> 5-7 large, very firm, red potatoes, chopped into smallish pieces. (Do NOT use potatoes that get mushy!)
>
> 2 large (28 oz) can diced tomatoes, not drained.
>
> 1 large can (28 oz.) kidney beans, not drained
>
> 1 standard can of kidney beans, not drained.

Directions
1. Brown sausage with onions in a big soup pot. When browned, I drain to reduce the grease.
2. Add tomatoes and kidney beans to meat and onions, bring to a simmer.
3. Add chopped potatoes and cook gently until the potatoes are tender.

You can correct the seasonings, but I find that the flavoring of the hot sausage is usually enough.

Tasty, and matures and freezes well so I make large batches. Great on a cold day with crusty French bread or toasted whole grain bread.

Chicken Potato Soup
Linda Warren

Many years ago my husband had the flu and when he felt better he wanted homemade chicken noodle soup. I didn't have any noodles. When I informed him of this, his reply was to use anything. I got a chicken breast and two thighs out of the freezer and put it in the sink to thaw. For the next two hours I kept wondering what I was going to put in it. I had rice and I thought of using that, but I settled on potatoes. I added the rest of the ingredients to give it more taste. My husband loved it! If he thinks he's catching a cold, he'll say make that soup with the potatoes in it.

Ingredients
Boil chicken breast and 2 Thighs (with skin and bone).
½ onion
3 or 4 green onions.
14.5 oz can diced tomatoes
Potatoes (white – peel and cut up about 3 medium into small pieces) Add more if you like.
1 tsp Chicken powder or 2 cubes of Chicken bouillon
1 bay leaf
Salt and pepper to taste

Directions
1. Boil chicken in big pot with salt and pepper and a little onion. When done (about 2 hours), remove chicken. Let cool and then remove bones and skin. Cut up.

2. Add the next ingredients to pot and stir. If it's cooked down add a 14.5 oz can of chicken broth or water. Cook until potatoes are soft. And then add the cut up chicken. Stir gently.

Enjoy!

***

Two time Rita® nominated and best-selling author Linda Warren has written fifty books for Harlequin. A native Texan, she married her high school sweetheart and they live on a lake in central Texas. He fishes and she writes. Works perfect.

Hubby's Gumbo
Linda Warren

When I married my husband, his mother would always bring him Gumbo for his birthday. I asked her many times what was in it because it was so good, but I never wrote it down. She passed away in 2010. I didn't think until weeks later that there would be no more gumbo. No one in the family had the recipe. I guess we assumed she would live forever. My husband's birthday was fast approaching and I knew he expected me to make it. I tried to bribe him with a new rod and reel. He said no. He wanted gumbo. I remembered some of the ingredients and the rest I added what I thought would taste good. After some adjustments and a couple of headaches, it turned out great. I am now the official gumbo maker.

Ingredients
    1 lb Shrimp (medium size - peel and devein)
    Chicken (I use a breast and two thighs with skin and bone –
        boil & cut up)
    Sausage (any kind you like – boil and cut up)
    4 oz. Crab meat
    3 Slices of bacon
    1 Green Bell pepper
    1 Onion
    3 Cloves of Garlic
    1 Sm. can of tomato sauce
    16 oz frozen cut up Okra
    ½ tsp. chili powder
    1 Bay leaf (1 big or 2 small)
    Gumbo File – about 1 Tbsp or more. Depends on taste.
    Broth from boiling chicken and 14.5 can of broth.

171

2 Tbsp Flour
2 Tbsp Oil
Tony Cachere's Creole seasoning – to taste
Salt and pepper to taste

Directions

1. Boil chicken and sausage. Cut up. (Usually do this a day ahead)
2. Rinse crab meat really well.
3. In a big pot add 2 Tbsps of flour and 2 Tbsps of oil (olive or veg) Mix until fully combined. Makes a roux.
4. In a frying pan brown cut up bacon and then add cut up onion and cut up green pepper. Sauté until tender and then add garlic.
5. Keep stirring roux. When it's the color you like, add tomato sauce and sautéed onion and pepper. Mix well. Add broth, bay leaf, gumbo file and chili powder. Let simmer on medium. May have to add a little water if too thick
6. Boil okra. When al dente add to mixture.
7. Add salt and pepper to taste, shrimp, chicken, sausage and crab. Sprinkle in TCC seasoning (I add just a little to keep it from getting too salty). Stir gently and let simmer until shrimp is done.

Serve over rice. Delicious!

Kimberly Kincaid's Souper Easy Pumpkin Apple Soup
Tracy Brogan

This recipe is special to me because I got it from my dear friend, author Kimberly Kincaid. She and I started our writing journeys around the same time, and I don't think I would have lasted through those first few years without her support and expert advice! I'm not sure I would have made it from wannabe writer to published author without her. She's a great cook, a talented writer, and a fabulous friend.

Ingredients
1 15 oz. can of pumpkin
2 cups chicken broth (You can also use vegetable broth)
¾ cup whole milk
½ tsp. apple pie spice
2 Tbs. maple syrup
1 large apple cut into bite size pieces
5 slices cooked, crispy, crumbled bacon. (This is optional.)

Directions
1. Warm the pumpkin and broth in a stockpot stir until smooth.
2. Add the other ingredients and heat (don't boil) for five or so minutes until the apple begins to soften.
3. When I make this, I also add ½ cup of sauteed finely diced onions and carrots just to get a few more veggies into my kids!
4. I garnish it with crispy fried onions and chopped pecans. Yum!

***

Tracy Brogan is the *USA Today*, *Wall Street Journal*, and Amazon bestselling author of both the Bell Harbor and Trillium Bay series. Her debut novel, *Crazy Little Thing*, has sold more than a million copies, and her books have been translated into more than a dozen languages. A three-time finalist for the Romance Writers of America RITA® Award, she writes fun, funny stories full of family, laughter, and love. Brogan lives in Michigan.

Texas Chili- Absolutely No Beans Allowed
Nancy C. Weeks

I have no doubt that it's against the law to put beans in Texas chili. This law may be buried deep in a dust-caked law book stuck behind hundreds of other old books, but the law is the law. Okay, maybe it not a law, but I married a tall, heart of gold, dear Texan man, and this is his mother's chili recipe. She shared it with me, and I've made it for him often over the last forty years. It's what kept our marriage a daily example of what happily ever after looks like. No beans allowed.

Ingredients
    2-pounds ground beef
    1 tsp ground cumin – or more is you love cumin
    3½ Tbs chili powder
    2 cloves of chopped garlic
    1 small onion chopped
    1 8 oz can tomato sauce
    3 C water
    2 Tbs. flour

Directions
1. Brown beef with onions. Add garlic and cook a couple more minutes. Add flour, chili powder, cumin, salt and pepper. Mix thoroughly. Add tomato sauce and water. Bring to a low boil and simmer for 40 minutes. Serve with chopped tomatoes, jalapenos, fresh onion, grated cheese
2. Soften twelve corn tortillas in the microwave for about 20 seconds. Spread a cup of chili on the bottom of a baking

dish. Place shredded cheese, a few sprinkles of raw, chopped onion in the lower third of the tortilla and roll. Place seam side down in a baking dish. It will not matter if the corn tortillas are not rolled perfectly. Pour chili over the top, cover with cheese and bake for about 20 minutes at 350 degrees until everything is gooey delicious.

Note: I make a double batch and freeze it. It is wonderful with grill hot dogs. I also use it for my Beef and Cheese Enchiladas.

***

Nancy C. Weeks writes romantic suspense novels that sometimes have a touch of the supernatural. Her characters stalk her dreams until she curls up with her laptop and creates riveting tales sure to end with the most satisfying HEA.

Bacon and Lentil Soup
Toni Anderson

This is a delicious soup I've been making for years, based on an old Delia Smith recipe (Delia is the original goddess of British cooking in my eyes). I love making double or triple batches in the autumn and freezing it for future lunches on cold weekends. I've noticed my characters rarely cook–they are usually too busy running from danger or solving crimes! If you have a food processor now is the time to drag it out of the cupboard and give it a good workout.

INGREDIENTS:
    6 bacon rashers, chopped
    6 oz whole green-brown lentils (175g), washed and drained (you can also use split red lentils).
    1 tablespoon olive oil
    2 large carrots, chopped
    1 large onion, chopped
    3 stalks of celery, sliced
    Tin tomatoes (225g)
    3 cloves garlic, crushed
    3 pints good quality vegetable stock (1.75 litres)
    8 oz savoy cabbage (225g), finely shredded (optional but delicious).
    2 tablespoons fresh parsley, chopped to serve.
    Salt and freshly milled black pepper

DIRECTIONS:

1. Heat the oil in a large cooking pot. Fry the bacon in the pot until it begins to brown. Stir in the carrots, onions and celery and with the heat fairly high, toss them around to brown them a little at the edges. Now stir in the washed, drained lentils plus the tomatoes along with the crushed garlic. Add the stock.
2. Let the soup come to the boil stirring regularly, then cover and simmer on a very low heat, for about an hour. About 15 minutes before the end add the cabbage. Season to taste. Just before serving give the soup a whirl with a hand-held blender (taking care not to get burnt!) and then sprinkle chopped parsley in the bowl.

(Serves 4-6 people) Dairy free, gluten free. Leave out the bacon for a vegan option!

***

Toni Anderson writes gritty, sexy, FBI Romantic Thrillers, and is a *New York Times* and a *USA Today* bestselling author. Her books have won the Readers' Choice, Aspen Gold, Book Buyers' Best, Golden Quill, and National Excellence in Romance Fiction awards. She's been a finalist in both the Vivian Contest and the RITA Award from the Romance Writers of America, and also in the Daphne du Maurier Award of Excellence. More than two million copies of her books have been downloaded.

Best known for her "COLD" books perhaps it's not surprising to discover Toni lives in one of the most extreme climates on earth-- Manitoba, Canada. Formerly a Marine Biologist, she still misses the ocean, but is lucky enough to travel for research purposes. In January 2016, she visited FBI Headquarters in Washington DC, including a tour of the Strategic Information and Operations Center. She hopes not to get arrested for her Google searches.

Chapter Seven
Quick Breads

Great–Grandma's Drop Biscuits
Collette Cameron

My mother made these biscuits all through my childhood which was a recipe her grandmother gave her. They've become a favorite of my family's too, and I cannot make chili, stew, or another hearty soup without making a double batch or my family complains.

This recipe dates to at least the middle 1800s and possibly before that. My Great-Grandmother's family was Norwegian, and she was a first-generation American. In fact, my great-great-grandmother was pregnant when with my great-grandma when she arrived in the United States.

Ingredients
2½ cups all-purpose flour
4 tsp baking powder
1 tsp salt
6 tablespoons shortening
1¼ cup cold milk

*If the dough is too dry, add a bit more milk. If it is too wet, add a bit more flour. It should not be stiff.

Directions
1. Preheat Oven to 425°
2. Mix all of the ingredients together until a smooth, wet dough forms. Drop by large tablespoon full onto an ungreased baking sheet.

3. Bake until golden brown-25-30 minutes. If you like your biscuits a little crisper, add extra shortening and bake longer.
4. Serve warm with butter, jam, or honey. They are delicious reheated the next day too.

***

USA Today Bestselling, award-winning author COLLETTE CAMERON® scribbles Scottish and Regency historical romance novels featuring dashing rogues, rakes, scoundrels, and the spirited heroines who reform them. Blessed with an overactive and witty muse that won't stop whispering new romantic romps in her ear, she's lived in Oregon her entire life. Although she dreams of living in Scotland part-time. A confessed Cadbury chocoholic, you'll always find a dash of inspiration and a pinch of humor in her sweet-to-spicy timeless romances®.

Southern Buttermilk Cornbread
Mindy Neff

Since I'm originally from the south—northern Louisiana—we cook a lot with bacon grease. I think that's what gives this cornbread such a great flavor. This recipe was handed down from my grandmother, to my mother, to me and now to my girls. Every holiday our turkey is accompanied by cornbread dressing. We don't stuff the bird, we just make it in a separate pan. It wouldn't be the holidays without cornbread dressing. Below is the recipe.

Ingredients
    1 cup white cornmeal
    ¼ cup Bisquick
    1 tsp baking powder
    1 tsp salt
    ½ tsp baking soda
    1 egg
    3 TBS bacon grease
    ¾ cup buttermilk

Directions
1. Mix dry ingredients and add egg and buttermilk.
2. In a cast iron skillet, heat the bacon grease until it smokes.
3. Pour hot bacon grease into the cornmeal mixture and stir.
4. Pour mixture back into the skillet and bake at 425 degrees for 25 minutes.

Almond Loaf
Tracy Brogan

Making this almond loaf always makes me happy. Partly because it's yummy but also because I got the recipe from a neighbor who brought me a loaf when I was a happy but anxious new mom who had just moved into a new house. We became fast friends and our daughters played together nearly every day. It was a wonderfully special time in my life and I'm still grateful for that friendship. Don't count the calories in this one. They don't matter!

Ingredients
    1 cup melted butter
    2 cups white sugar
    1 cup sour cream
    1 tsp. vanilla
    2 cups flour
    ¼ tsp. salt
    1 tsp baking power
    1 cup almond paste

Directions
1. Mix butter, sugar, eggs, sour cream, and vanilla.
2. Fold in sifted flour, salt, and baking power.
3. Mix in crumbled almond paste through the batter.
4. Pour batter in greased angel food cake pan or two small loaf pans.
5. Bake at 350 degrees for 1 hour. Cool in pan for 10 minutes.

Optional: Drizzle a frosting of powdered sugar and milk over cooled cake if desired.

ROYAL BANANA NUT BREAD
Teri Wilson

This recipe is a modified version of a banana bread I've been making for almost thirty years! When I read that Meghan Markle made homemade banana on a royal tour to Australia and added ginger and chocolate chips, I toyed with my old stand-by banana bread recipe and came up with this special royal version.

Ingredients
- ½ cup shortening
- 1 cup sugar
- 2 eggs
- 3 mashed bananas
- 3 tablespoons vanilla yogurt
- 1 tablespoon lemon juice
- 2 cups flour
- ½ teaspoon baking powder
- 1 teaspoon salt
- ½ baking soda
- ½ cup chocolate chips
- 1 teaspoon fresh grated ginger
- 1 teaspoon cinnamon

Directions
1. Cream shortening and sugar.
2. Beat in eggs, then bananas, yogurt, fresh ginger and lemon juice.
3. Mix dry ingredients and cinnamon. Add to banana mixture. Stir just to dampen flour.

4. Fold in chocolate chips.
5. Pour into 9 x 5 x 3 loaf pan sprayed with Pam.
6. Bake at 350 degrees for 1 hour. Cool for 10 minutes then remove from pan.

Irish Brown Bread
Melanie Greene

I married an Irishman and spent a long time combing through brown bread recipes and converting from metric in search of one I could make in America that turned out as delicious as that of my sister-in-law in Dublin. This one I cobbled together is our family favorite, until we visit our relatives and something about Irish ingredients and her baking skill puts me in second place again.

Ingredients
1⅓ cups all-purpose flour
2⅜ cups whole wheat flour
½ cup wheat bran
½ cup wheatgerm (or ground flaxseed meal)
2¼ tsp baking powder
1 tsp salt
1 tsp treacle (or Golden Syrup or blackstrap molasses)
3 cups milk

Directions
1. Preheat the oven to 475° and prepare your loaf pan with a hearty coat of spray oil.
2. Mix the dry ingredients in a large bowl - no sifting required.
3. Add the treacle and at least 2 cups of the milk, adding more milk until your mixture is moist and not watery.
4. Add dough to loaf pan and bake at 475° for 20 minutes.

Without opening the oven, reduce the heat to 300° and bake for one more hour.

5. Check the bottom of your loaf; if it sounds hollow when tapped, it's done. If it needs a bit more baking, add it back to the oven for another 10-15 minutes.

Wonderful with fresh butter, soup, smoked salmon, or on its own.

***

Melanie Greene lives in a small cottage in a big city and writes contemporary romance featuring lots of laughter and love.

Massa
Brenda Margriet

Massa is a sweet bread that my Portuguese mother-in-law made every Easter and Christmas. I have taken over the tradition. At Easter, hardboiled eggs are buried in the dough and baked inside the bread.

(Makes 2 loaves using round pans 9 inches in diameter and 3 inches deep)

Ingredients
   1 c. milk
   Zest of 1 lemon
   2 tbsp yeast
   ¼ c. warm water
   1 c. sugar
   1 tsp salt
   3 eggs
   3 c. flour* (total of 5 – 6 c. needed – see additional
      measurement below)
   ½ c. butter, softened
   2-3 c. flour*
   1 egg

Directions
1. Warm milk and lemon zest, being careful not to bring to a boil. Set aside.

2. In a LARGE bowl, dissolve yeast in warm water. While milk is cooling, let yeast start to work.
3. Once milk is cool, add to yeast mixture. Stir in sugar, eggs, salt, butter and 3 cups of flour. Beat until smooth. Stir in enough of the remaining flour to make the dough easy to handle. Knead dough on a lightly floured surface until smooth and elastic (about 5 minutes).
4. Place in a greased bowl and let rise in a warm place until it is double in size (about 1 to 1.5 hours).
5. Punch down dough and divide into 10 "bun" size pieces. Grease round pans and arrange in in a flower pattern (5 to a pan).
6. Cover and let rise until double (about an hour). The longer you let rise at this stage, the lighter the bread will be. May need to leave longer than the hour.
7. Beat remaining egg and brush over tops of loaves.
8. Bake in 325F oven until golden brown, about 35 – 45 minutes.

***

Brenda Margriet writes savvy, slow burn, contemporary romances with ordinarily amazing characters. In her own ordinarily amazing life, she had a successful career in radio and television production before deciding to pilfer from her retirement plan to support her writing compulsion.

Readers have called her stories "poignant," "explicit and steamy," "interesting, intriguing and entertaining," and "unlike any romance you've read before" (she assumes the latter was meant in a good way).

Lemon Bread
Stephanie J. Scott

When I think about family recipes, a common theme comes to mind: dessert. While I was well into my 20s before I discovered a fondness for cooking, I learned to bake early on. I have so many memories of baking in between rounds of card games with my mom on rainy Sunday afternoons, of mixing up cookie batter with my grandma and aunts in a busy kitchen, and while visiting with cousins. I was definitely the only one out of my college room-mates who stocked Crisco in our cupboard for just this purpose.

A regular dessert at family events is my mom's lemon bread. I asked her recently where the recipe came from since it had always been made from a recipe card rather than a cookbook. A family friend brought the bread and the recipe to what would have been my grandparents' fiftieth wedding anniversary, had my grandfather not passed away six months prior. We had the party anyway, rebranding it an open house. Guests didn't seem to come and go-they stayed. For hours. I was a tween at the time, and helped make photo displays on posterboard (ah, the days before digital slideshows!). This bread connected to that memory makes sense why we've continued to serve it time and again.

Directions
    1 cup sugar
    ½ cup milk
    ½ cup oil
    2 eggs
    Grated rind of one lemon
    1 tsp baking powder

1 ½ cups flour
1 tsp salt
½ cup chopped nuts (optional)

Top Glaze

Juice of one lemon
¼ cup sugar

Directions

1. Set oven to 350 degrees.
2. Mix wet ingredients together in a bowl.
3. Assemble dry ingredients separately, then mix with wet.
4. Pour into a small loaf pan and bake for 1 hour.
5. While still warm, pour the glaze over the top and let cool.

***

Stephanie J. Scott writes young adult and romance about characters who put their passions first. Her debut ALTERATIONS about a fashion-obsessed loner who reinvents herself was a Romance Writers of America RITA® award finalist. She enjoys dance fitness, everything cats, and has a slight obsession with Instagram. A Midwest girl at heart, she resides outside of Chicago with her tech-of-all-trades husband and fuzzy furbabies.

Sweet Potato Cornbread
Aliza Mann

I still remember the first time I had this dish. My mom gave a hot slice of it with no accompaniment, save a pat of butter. One bit and I thought my mom was a master chef. Fortunately, the recipe is easy enough for all of us to be master chefs.

Ingredients:
    1 cup of roasted sweet potatoes (1 large or two small)
    ½ cup olive oil
    2 cups cornmeal
    1 cup (all purpose) flour
    ¼ cup brown sugar
    ½ teaspoon baking soda
    1 teaspoon salt
    1 teaspoon apple pie seasoning (or mix 1/3 tsp of each: cinnamon, nutmeg, all spice)
    4 large eggs (room temperature)
    1 ½ cups buttermilk
    ¼ cup honey
    1 stick (8 tablespoons) melted butter

Directions:
1. Preheat oven to 375 degrees F.
2. Roast sweet potatoes
3. Wash potatoes thoroughly with skin on.
4. Baste with olive oil. If you need a little more to coat the potatoes, don't worry.
5. Place in heated oven on a baking sheet for 35 - 45 minutes or until

potatoes are completely soft inside. Use a fork to test. When done, the fork will easily slide into the potato.

6. Once done, set aside to cool.
7. Using a cast iron skillet, warm butter until melted. Set aside.
8. In a large mixing bowl, whisk together cornmeal, flour, brown sugar, baking powder, baking soda, salt, and apple pie spice.
9. In a medium bowl, whisk together mashed sweet potatoes (scoop the flesh from the skin and add to bowl), melted butter, buttermilk, honey, then eggs last.
10. Pour blended wet mixture into dry ingredients and stir until just combined. Ensure the spoon scrapes the bottom and side of the bowl to prevent clumps of dry mix on the bottom.
11. Pour mixture into cast iron skillet and smooth the top with a spatula.
12. Place in the oven and bake until golden brown for 35 minutes. Use a fork or toothpick to test in the center. When done, the utensil will come out clean.
13. Serve cornbread in slices on a platter or right from the skillet, w/butter.

(Serves 8 – 10)

Recipe Notes:
- Pairs well with fried chicken and collard greens or can be served alone – warm with a pat of butter.
- The cast iron skillet is optional; however, it provides optimal results when baking any type of corn bread.

Too good for the bake sale Banana Bread...
Lisa Kessler

This is a family favorite, and no one will guess you made it from a box!

1. Start with a box mix and follow the directions on the label to make the batter.
2. Once it's mixed and smooth, mash up a quarter of a banana and add it.
3. Mix again, and then add half a bag of milk chocolate chips to the batter.
4. Bake as instructed on the box.

The chocolate will melt, and you'll be getting requests for more at every potluck.

I hope these hacks help my fellow non-cooks out there look like baking royalty!

***

Lisa Kessler is a Best-Selling author of paranormal fiction. She's a two-time San Diego Book Award winner for Best Published Fantasy-Sci-fi-Horror and Best Published Romance. Her books have also won the PRISM award, the Award of Excellence, the National Excellence in Romantic Fiction Award, the Award of Merit from the Holt Medallion, and an International Digital Award for Best Paranormal.

Her short stories have been published in print anthologies and magazines, and her vampire story, Immortal Beloved, was a finalist for a Bram Stoker award.

When she's not writing, Lisa is a professional vocalist, and has performed with San Diego Opera as well as other musical theater companies in San Diego.

Chapter Eight
Cookies

Kristan's World Famous Chocolate Chip Cookies
Kristan Higgins

Thanks to the voracious cookie eaters in my house, I can whip up the batter for these in under four minutes. They are crisp yet soft, buttery and delicious, a big hug in the form of a cookie. Every time the kids come home, or every time I'm visited by the little twins next door, I make these to the great delight of everyone.

Ingredients
2¼ cups of flour
1 teaspoon salt
1 teaspoon baking soda
Combined in a bowl.
2 sticks of butter, softened
1 cup of brown sugar
⅓ cup white sugar

Mix together in mixer till well combined.

Add:
2 eggs
2 teaspoons of vanilla

Directions
1. Add in dry ingredients. Mix till smooth.
2. Add 1 cup chocolate chips and 1 cup of peanut butter chips. Mix on low till combined.
3. Drop from small melon scoop onto greased cookie sheets.
4. Bake for 11-12 minutes at 375 degrees.

White Chocolate Fantasy Clusters
Blake Oliver

My husband's grandmother made these every Christmas.
You can't eat just one piece.

Ingredients:
- 4 c. Rice Chex cereal
- 2 c. pretzel sticks, coarsely broken
- 1 c. cashews, coarsely chopped
- ½ package (16-oz. size) vanilla-flavored candy coating
- ½ c. semisweet chocolate chips, melted

Directions:
1. Grease rectangular pan, 13x9x2 inches. Glass is best. Mix cereal, pretzels and cashews in large bowl; set aside. Melt candy coating in 2-quart saucepan over low heat, stirring constantly. Melting in the microwave is not recommended for this step.
2. Pour over cereal mixture, stirring until evenly coated. Press in pan, cool slightly.
3. Drizzle with melted chocolate chips; let stand until chocolate is firm. Break into clusters. Store in airtight container.

Makes about 24 clusters.

Grandma Cameron's Scottish Shortbread Cookies
Collette Cameron

Grandpa Cameron was descended from Scots that settled Nova Scotia, Canada, after the Great Clearings in Scotland in the mid-1700s. Grandpa immigrated to the United States from Nova Scotia as a child, and he adored buttery shortbread with strong tea. After testing recipes early in their marriage, Grandma finally created one that he said was perfect. I remember eating the crisp cookies as a child, and knowing how much I adored baking, Grandma shared the recipe with me. These shortbread cookies are a Christmas staple at my house.

Ingredients
2½ cups all-purpose flour
½ tsp salt
1 cup unsalted butter, room temperature. (Use high-quality butter.)
1 cup powdered sugar
1 tsp pure vanilla extract

Preheat oven to 350°

Cookies:
1. Combine flour and salt in a bowl using a wire whisk. Set aside.
2. Beat the butter until smooth. Add the sugar and vanilla. Beat until smooth.
3. Add flour mixture, and mix until a stiff dough forms.

4. Form into a flattened ball, wrap in plastic wrap and chill for ½ hour.
5. Roll dough out on a lightly floured surface until ¼" thick.
6. Using a floured cookie cutter, cut into shapes, then place on an ungreased baking sheet. Place the cookies back in the fridge for 15, so they keep their shapes better when baking.
7. Bake on the middle rack until the edges are golden brown. Remove and cool on wire racks.
8. Eat plain or decorate with melted chocolate, icing, and sprinkles.

Wedges:
1. Combine flour and salt. Set aside.
2. Beat the butter until smooth, and then add the sugar. Beat until creamy.
3. Mix the other dry ingredients together and then add to the butter mixture. Mix together until you have a stiff dough.
4. Press into a 9" round pan.
5. Bake on the middle rack until the edges are golden brown. Remove and cool before cutting.

Because I like my shortbread really crunchy, I'll cut mine into wedges while it's warm and then put those pieces on a cookie sheet. I return them to the oven for another 5-10 minutes.

I also like to dip one end in melted chocolate.

Yummy!!

***

USA Today Bestselling, award-winning author **COLLETTE CAMERON**® scribbles Scottish and Regency historical romance novels featuring dashing rogues, rakes, scoundrels, and the spirited heroines who reform them. Blessed with an overactive and witty muse that won't stop whispering new romantic romps in her ear, she's lived in Oregon her entire life. Although she dreams of living in Scotland part-time. A confessed Cadbury chocoholic, you'll always find a dash of inspiration and a pinch of humor in her sweet-to-spicy timeless romances®.

LAVENDER SUGAR COOKIES
Sheila Roberts

Ingredients:
- 2¾ cups flour
- 1 tsp baking soda
- ½ tsp baking powder
- 1½ cups (white) granulated sugar
- 1 cup butter, room temp and soft
- 1 egg
- 1 – 2 tsp dried lavender buds, crumbled (Note: lavender can be strong, so if you've never baked with it before I advise going easy the first time out, putting in a little at a time.)
- A little extra granulated sugar to roll your cookies in

Directions:
1. Preheat oven to 350
2. Cream together butter and sugar until smooth, then add egg.
3. Sift in dry ingredients gradually, adding crumbled lavender and mixing as you go.
4. Roll into small (1 inch) balls, then roll in sugar and place on ungreased cookie sheet.
5. Bake 10 minutes (may be more or a little less, depending on your oven).
6. Let stand on cookie sheet two minutes, then move to cookie rack to cool.

***

With nearly thirty books to her name, **Sheila Roberts** is a frequent USA Today and Publishers Weekly bestseller - and a fan favorite. Her Christmas perennial "On Strike for Christmas" was made into a movie for the Lifetime Channel and her novel "The Nine Lives of Christmas" was made into a movie for Hallmark. Her novel "Angel Lane" was listed as one of Amazon's Best Books of the Year. Before settling into her writing career, Sheila owned a singing telegram company and played in band. When she's not traveling, Sheila splits her time between the Pacific Northwest and Southern California.

Monster Cookies
Tracy Brogan

This recipe was very trendy when I was a kid and I remember making them with my oldest sister. We thought it was hilarious to make such a huge batch and since they had basically every ingredient, they were like all of our favorites mixed into one cookie. This recipe is also special to me because a friend gave me a box of handwritten recipes as a wedding gift, and this was one of them.

Ingredients
>1 lb. butter
>2 lbs. brown sugar
>4 cups white sugar
>8 tsp. baking soda
>2 tsp. vanilla
>12 eggs
>3 lbs. peanut butter
>16 oz. chocolate chips
>16 oz. chopped nuts
>18 cups quick oatmeal
>16 oz. M&M's

Directions
1. In a VERY large bowl, mix butter, sugars, baking soda, and vanilla until creamy.
2. Add eggs.
3. Mix in peanut butter.

Cookies

4. Add all the other ingredients and mix thoroughly.
5. Using a cookie scooper, drop the batter onto cookie sheets and bake at 350 degrees for 8-10 minutes.

Batter may be frozen in small amounts for future use. There is no flour in this recipe. Just oatmeal.

Pumpkin Walnut Spice Biscotti
JoMarie DeGioia

Caroline Richmond tests out some new recipes in her bakery Sweet Escape for the Fall Festival in Dreaming Eli, one of the books in my Cypress Corners series of Contemporary Romantic Comedies. Eli Graham nicknames her "Cupcake" so Caro can't resist calling him "Graham Cracker!" Feel free to experiment with the cinnamon and spices to make these your own.

Create Sweet Escape's signature biscotti and bake a taste of Autumn!

Ingredients
1 cup sugar
4 Tbsp butter or margarine, softened
½ cup pumpkin pie filling
1 large egg
1½ tsp vanilla extract
3 cups all-purpose flour
2 Tbsp pumpkin spice
2 tsp baking powder
½ tsp salt
1 tsp cinnamon
¾ cup chopped walnuts
1 beaten egg (for egg wash)

Icing
½ cup white chocolate chips

Directions
1. Preheat oven to 375F and line a cookie sheet with parchment paper.

2. In large mixing bowl or stand mixer beat together sugar, butter or margarine, and pumpkin pie filling until light and fluffy.
3. Add egg and mix until combined.
4. Stir in vanilla extract.
5. In separate bowl whisk together flour, pumpkin spice, baking powder, salt, and cinnamon.
6. Gradually add flour mixture to pumpkin mixture, mixing on low speed.
7. Stir in walnuts and mix until evenly distributed.
8. Turn dough out onto prepared baking sheet in two mounds.
9. Form dough into two 10"x3" logs and flatten slightly.
10. Brush with beaten egg wash.
11. Bake 25 minutes.
12. Remove from oven (don't turn oven off) and allow to cool for 20 minutes.
13. Once biscotti has cooled, lift parchment paper holding baked loaves onto a cutting board and line cookie sheet with a fresh sheet of parchment paper.
14. Cut biscotti loaves diagonally into ¾" slices and place cut-side down onto prepared cookie sheet.
15. Bake at 350F for another 12-15 minutes until biscotti is dry.
16. Remove from oven and allow to cool completely.
17. Prepare icing by melting white chocolate in microwave-safe bowl at 10-second increments, stirring frequently, until melted.
18. Spread or drizzle melted chocolate over biscotti, over the top or on one side.
19. Allow chocolate to cool/harden before serving.

***

JoMarie DeGioia is a bestselling author of Historical and Contemporary Romance and an RWA Honor Roll Author. She is the author of nearly 50 Romances, and writes Young Adult Fantasy/Adventure stories and Paranormal Romance too. She divides her time between Central Florida and New England.

Cadbury Cookies
Sarah Andre

We make these only at Christmastime because they are SO delicious that if we made them throughout the year we'd be stars in our own morbidly obese reality show. I promise, you will be asked for this recipe <u>every</u> time you make them!

My husband and I came across a version of these in Ireland, where they're called Millionaire Bars. There was a thick layer of caramel between their shortbread cookie base and the chocolate.

Preheat oven to 350°

Ingredients
    1C softened butter (we use Land O Lakes, salted.)
    1C light brown sugar
    2C flour
    1 egg yolk
    5 large Cadbury milk chocolate bars, broken into their
        individual squares.

Directions
1. In a mixer, combine the first 4 ingredients. Dough will be a thick, shortbread texture.
2. Using your fingers press the cookie base in a thin, even layer on a greased 9" x 14" or 10" x 15" cookie sheet.
3. Bake 12-15 min, until top is a light brown.

4. Remove from oven, and turn off oven. Quickly lay the chocolate squares all over the top, then return to the still-hot oven for 30-45 sec. Remove, place pan on a cooling rack and spread the now-melted chocolate evenly over the top. Leave overnight to cool and harden. Cut into 1 inch squares.

Option: Crush a few Heath bars and sprinkle on the still-cooling chocolate for an even richer taste.

Option: Obviously, you can top with any chocolate bars you like- my mom used to buy Hershey's, but Cadbury gives the cookies an amazingly creamy flavor.

***

Sarah Andre is a 2017 RITA® finalist, which is Romance Writers of America highest award of distinction. She lives in serene Southwest FL with her husband and two naughty Pomeranians. When she's not writing, Sarah is either reading novels, exercising to rude alternative rock music or coloring. Yes, you heard right. She's all over those coloring books for adults.

Aunt Dixie's Divinity
Jodi Thomas

(written on the back of an envelope with a birthday card inside.)

If the recipe turns out, I serve it at Christmas!!

1. Put in a quart size pan---works best in heavy pan, medium heat: 2 cups sugar ½ cup water Dash of salt
2. Bring to a boil---should be rolling boil but not a crazy boil that climbs up the sides of the pan are you'll have a mess.
3. Boil stirring most of the time and watching ALL the time for about 6 to 8 minutes until the mixture will go soft ball stage. (That means when you drop a drop of it in a small bowl of cold water, you can push it around with your finger and make a sloppy ball.) Once that happens, I usually let it boil for another minute just to make sure it's ready.
4. Next: Pour over marshmallow cream from a small jar 8 ounces, and start to mix on low for about 30 seconds, then kick it up to high for about 4-6 minutes. Sometime during this add 1 teaspoon of vanilla.
5. Stop mixing when the it starts to thicken, losses it's shine, or the ripples the mixer makes stay up for three seconds.
6. Add a cup of chopped nuts and make a few more rounds with the mixer

Or

Wait and add a nut on top of each piece. May also add a cherry on top if you don't like nuts.

Late: Using two spoons, drop candy on waxed paper. If the first few drops go flat, slow down a bit and give the candy time to cool a minute. Once the candy looks right coming of the spoon, move fast.

This makes about three dozen candies. The first few will be flat, but they still taste just as good. The last few may be stiff so eat them first.

If you decide to put the nut or cherry on top be sure to dry the cherries on a paper towel first and put them on as soon as you drop all the candy.

Never double the recipe. It won't turn out.

Love you, kid, and remember, divinity is like birthdays, not everyone turns out perfect.

~ Aunt Dixie Kirkland

***

Jodi Thomas is a certified marriage and family counselor, a fifth generation Texan, a Texas Tech graduate, and writer-in-residence at West Texas A&M University. She lives in Amarillo, Texas.

White Chocolate Raspberry Thumbprints
Shirley Jump

Ingredients
½ cup butter
½ cup shortening
½ cup granulated sugar
½ cup powdered sugar
½ teaspoon baking soda
½ teaspoon cream of tartar
⅛ teaspoon salt
1 egg
½ teaspoon vanilla
2 cups all-purpose flour
⅓ cup seedless raspberry jam
1 cup white chocolate chips
Red sugar sprinkles

Directions
1. In a large mixing bowl, beat the butter and the shortening with an electric mixer (or use a stand mixer and let the machine do the work), then add the sugar, powdered sugar, baking soda, cream of tartar, and the salt. Beat just until combined.
2. Add the egg and vanilla, then mix in the flour gradually.
3. Cover the dough and refrigerate for three hours. I know, it's a long wait, but it'll be worth it later.
4. Heat the oven to 375 degrees.
5. Roll the dough into ¾-inch balls and put them on an ungreased cookie sheet.

213

6. With your thumb or the end of a wooden spoon, press a circular indentation into the center of each cookie.
7. Drop a ¼ teaspoon of jam into each thumbprint.
8. Bake cookies for 8-10 minutes, then cool on a wire rack for 5 minutes.
9. Put the white chocolate chips in a microwave-safe bowl and microwave on high in 30-second bursts, stirring each time, until the chips are melted.
10.   Pour the white chocolate into a resealable plastic bag and snip off a tiny bit of one corner. Drizzle the white chocolate over the cookies.
11.   Sprinkle cookies with red sugar to add that festive flair.

Makes three dozen, just enough for you and a very special, handsome friend!

Salted Caramel Shortbread Cookies
Shirley Jump

Ingredients
1 14-ounce can sweetened condensed milk
kosher salt
3 sticks butter (3/4 pound), unsalted, room temperature
1 cup sugar, plus a tablespoon or two extra set aside
1 teaspoon vanilla
3½ cups flour
¼ teaspoon salt

Directions
First, make the caramel.
1. Preheat the oven to 425 degrees.
2. Pour the condensed milk into a pie plate, stir in 1/4 teaspoon kosher salt, and cover it tightly with foil.
3. Put the pie plate in a big roasting pan, and fill it halfway up the pie plate with hot water.
4. Bake for 1 to 1¼ hours, adding more water if necessary.
5. Let cool, then whisk until smooth. It's delicious, by the way, but try not to eat it all because the cookies are so much more amazing when you add salted caramel.

Meanwhile, make the cookies.
1. Set the oven to 350 degrees.
2. The butter has to be room temp for this to work well,

so what I do is set the butter out first thing in the morning, make the caramel, then about 15 minutes before the caramel is done, I mix the cookie dough.

3. Cream the butter and sugar in a mixer.
4. Add the vanilla.
5. Mix the salt with the flour, then add the dry ingredients a little at a time and mix until the dough comes together.
6. I formed the dough into square logs (though you can make it into a plate shape and roll it out; I just hate doing cut-out cookies).
7. Wrap in plastic wrap and refrigerate 30 minutes.
8. Slice or cut the dough into 1/4- to 1/2-inch-thick cookies (mine were like 1/3 an inch). They don't spread much, so you can get quite a few on an ungreased cookie sheet.
9. Sprinkle with reserved sugar.
10. Bake for 20-24 minutes, switching the cookie sheets halfway through to get even cooking. Keep an eye on them because they go from perfect to burned fast.
11. Put wax paper under your cooling rack.
12. Remove cookies from the oven, place on the cooling racks.
13. Heat the caramel for 30 seconds in the microwave, then put it in a Ziploc bag and snip one end (to make a homemade pastry bag). Drizzle cookies with caramel, then sprinkle with kosher salt.

Eat. Repeat ;-)

***

When she's not writing books, New York Times and USA Today bestselling author **Shirley Jump** competes in triathlons, mostly because all that training lets her justify mid-day naps and a second slice of chocolate cake. She's published more than 75 books in 24 languages, although she's too geographically challenged to find any of those countries on a map.

Triple Ginger Cream Cookies
Piper G. Huguley

This combination of spice and buttercream goes back to the colonial times in the United States. However, according to the Betty Crocker Cooky book, published in 1963, this is the cookie of the 1910's because of the small amount of sugar used and more molasses as a sweetener. They really reached a heyday during World War 2 because it's a cookie that ships well. The low amount of sugar used meant that people could have something sweet to eat even though sugar was rationed. We've made this cookie for decades as a Christmas cookie but it works year round. I've made some tweaks to the basic Betty Crocker recipe. I think my mother would be pleased.

Yield: 3 dozen cookies

Ingredients
⅓ cup shortening
½ cup sugar
1 egg
½ cup molasses (Grandma's is the brand I like)
½ cup cold black coffee
2 cups all-purpose flour
1 teaspoon ground ginger
1 tablespoon crystallized ginger, chopped fine
1 tablespoon ginger paste
½ teaspoon salt
½ teaspoon baking soda
½ teaspoon nutmeg
½ teaspoon cloves
½ teaspoon cinnamon

217

Directions

1. Mix thoroughly shortening, sugar, egg, molasses and water. Blend in remaining ingredients. Cover. Chill at least 1 hour.
2. Heat oven to 400 degrees. Drop dough by teaspoonfuls 2 inches apart on parchment-lined baking sheet. Bake 8 minutes or until almost no imprint remains when touched with a finger. Immediately remove from the baking sheet and cool before you frost them with Buttercream Frosting.

Buttercream Frosting

(You could buy this in the store as vanilla frosting, but homemade is better.)

Ingredients

⅓ cup softened butter
3 cups confectioner's sugar
1½ teaspoons vanilla
About 2 tablespoons milk

Directions

1. Blend butter and sugar.
2. Stir in vanilla and milk. Beat until frosting is smooth and you can spread it on a cooled ginger cookie.

Variation: Ginger goes well with lemon and orange so if you want the frosting to be orange or lemon flavored then omit the vanilla and substitute orange (or lemon) juice for the milk. You can also add 2 teaspoons of orange peel or ½ teaspoon lemon peel if desired. Once you have frosted all of the ginger cookies, wait until the tops airdry before you stack them and send them to a loved one–if you are afraid you might eat them all yourself.

***

Piper G. Huguley is a two-time Golden Heart® finalist and author of two historical romance series: "Migrations of the Heart", about the Great Migration and "Home to Milford College." Her contemporary romance debut comes out in 2021 with Hallmark Publishing. She will make her historical fiction debut in March 2022 with William Morrow with a book about Ann Lowe, the Black fashion designer of Jackie Kennedy's wedding dress.

Rum Balls
Jo McNally

Let me tell you a secret... I married really well. Oh, it's not that he's a secret billionaire or a rugged cowboy or anything. But he COOKS. Back in my corporate days, I'd often come home to a fully-cooked meal (and on Fridays, a cocktail waiting on the counter). Like I said--I married well. He's a keeper, and I guess he feels the same about me, as we celebrated 25 years of marriage this year.

Does my Boston-Irish hubby influence my fictional heroes? Of course--especially my Irish hero, Finn, in *Barefoot on a Starlit Night*. Himself gave me side-eye more than once while reading when he saw that Finn borrowed some of his best lines!

I don't use my cooking muscles all that often, but I do have a few reliable recipes that get requested on a regular basis, and this is one of them. Even better? It doesn't require *cooking* at all! I am all about keeping things simple. Your hands might get a little messy while shaping--take your rings off first. These are best after they've sat for a few days, so try to do them 3-4 days ahead.

Whenever I serve these rum balls, people (especially men!) will say they can "feel" the booze, and they'll insist they're getting drunk. It's as if they think they're getting away with being naughty! But there's only a half cup of rum in the whole recipe, so even if they ate all four dozen cookies, they'd hardly be drunk! But... you may want to keep them away from the kiddies (the rum balls, not the men).

Ingredients:
    3 cups finely crushed vanilla wafers (about 75)
    2 cups powdered sugar
    1 cup finely chopped pecans (or walnuts)

¼ cup baking cocoa
¼ cup light corn syrup
½ cup light rum
Granulated sugar for coating

Directions
1. Mix crushed wafers, powdered sugar, pecans and cocoa.
2. Stir in rum and corn syrup.
3. Shape mixture into 1-inch balls.
4. Roll in granulated sugar.
5. Refrigerate in a tightly-covered container for several days before serving (I layer them with wax paper in between).

Makes 3-4 dozen.

These can also be made with brandy, and a friend just told me she made them with creme de menthe, which sounds delicious!

Leslie's Lemon Bars
Leslie Hachtel

I think the base of this recipe came from an old cookbook and it was changed and modified over the years. I use my hands for much of this recipe. It's messy but the bars come out better. And yes, I wash my hands before I mix.

Ingredients:
1⅓ cups + 2 Tbs. white flour
½ tsp. salt
½ cup Crisco
2-3 Tbs. water
⅓ cup butter
1 cup + 1 Tbs. white sugar
2 eggs
1¼ Tbs. grated lemon peel
¼ cup lemon juice

Directions
1. Mix 1-1/3 cups flour with salt and 1 Tbs. sugar and add shortening. Mix with a pastry dough blender (or your hands) until the particles are the size of small peas. Set aside about 1/3 cup for topping.
2. Then mix in water until dough will hold together.
3. Press into ungreased 9" x13" pan until uniform and about ¼ inch up on the sides of the pan.
4. In mixing bowl, add butter with 1 cup sugar and mix on slow speed until smooth.
5. Slowly add in eggs, 2 Tbs. flour, lemon peel and juice. Blend well.

Mixture may curdle but that is fine.

6. Pour into pastry lined pan and sprinkle with remaining crust mixture.

7. Bake at 400 degrees 30-35 minutes or until edges are dark golden brown. Cool completely before cutting.

Fresh Fruit Cookie Bars
Leslie Hachtel

I bought too many plums once and they were very ripe, so I decided to bake them into this pastry. You can also use peaches or thinly sliced apples or even pears. Or use your imagination.

Ingredients:
2 cups + ¼ cup flour
1 tsp. salt
¾ cup Crisco
4-5 Tbs. water
½ cup + 1 Tbs. white sugar
½ cup brown sugar, firmly packed
¼ tsp. cinnamon
About 4 cups ripe plums, thinly sliced apples, ripe peaches or thinly sliced pears

Directions:
1. Combine two cups flour with salt and 1 Tbs. white sugar.
2. Drop in Crisco and mix with pastry dough blender (or your clean hands) until particles are the size of small peas. Set aside one cup of mixture.
3. To the remainder, mix in water just until dough will hold together.
4. Press into ungreased 9"x13" pan until uniform and about ¼ inch up on the sides of the pan.
5. Mix fruit with white sugar and place on top of pastry.
6. Combine reserved crust mixture with brown sugar, ¼ cup flour and cinnamon and sprinkle over fruit.

Cookies

7. Place pan on foil lined cookie sheet since fruit will run.
8. Bake at 400 degrees for 35-40 minutes or until fruit is soft and top of crust and edges are golden brown.
9. Cool completely before cutting and store leftovers (if there are any) in refrigerator.

***

Leslie Hachtel is a bestselling author with sixteen published romance novels. They range from romantic suspense to paranormal to historical.

Mom's Winter Solstice Cookies
Cathryn Marr

My mom loved to bake and after years of creating and testing recipes she began writing a monthly cooking newsletter featuring down-home recipes. As a young woman I learned a great deal helping my mom with the newsletters, but it's the time we spent together in her kitchen, talking, and laughing, that's the most precious to me.

Every year my mom made these cookies for the winter solstice and served them with hot chocolate or mulled apple cider. I remember her saying the shortest day and longest night of the year should have its own cookie. I wholeheartedly and lovingly agree!

Ingredients
   2 cups packed brown sugar
   1 ½ cups butter, softened
   1 egg, beaten
   1 tsp. baking powder
   ¾ tsp. salt
   1 tsp. cinnamon
   ½ tsp. ground ginger
   ½ tsp. ground cloves
   3 ½ cups all-purpose flour

Directions
1. Cream sugar and butter until light and fluffy.
2. Beat in egg, and stir in baking powder, salt, and spices.
3. Stir flour into creamed mixture and mix well. (Dough might be stiff and I often finish by working the last of the flour in by hand.)

Cookies

4. On a lightly floured surface, roll dough to 1/4" thick.
5. Cut into desired shapes and top each cookie with a slivered almond.
6. Place on ungreased cookie sheet and bake at 350 degrees for 12-15 minutes.
7. Cool for one minute then move to a wire rack to finish cooling.

***

I write paranormal romantic suspense with my writing partner, Terese Ramin, under the pseudonym **Cathryn Marr**. **Soul Keeper (Brotherhood of Shadows)** is our first novel together, followed by **Emily's Halloween**, and **Gift of the Magpie**, a Christmas novella. Our second book, **Soul Bound**, will be released in 2022. Terese has been in the writing business for thirty years and published many books under her own name. And, like my mom, she's another woman I'm blessed to work with!

Easy-Peasy Buckeyes
Terri Osburn

For those who don't know (and who clearly did not grow up in Ohio) Buckeyes are chocolate covered peanut butter balls which resemble the nuts that fall from the buckeye tree (Aesculus glabra) that is so common in Ohio. As chocolate and peanut is my favorite combination of all time, I was ecstatic when I stumbled across a ridiculously simple hack to making these a few years ago. The manual labor of dipping them in the chocolate is the only somewhat strenuous part, but I assure you they are totally worth the effort. (Obviously, those with nut allergies will want to avoid this one.)

Ingredients:
   16 oz White frost ing (white not vanilla)
   10 oz Peanut butter chips
   12 oz Chocolate chips

Directions:
1. Melt the peanut butter chips in the microwave. Check every 20 seconds or less and keep stirring to make sure they don't burn.
2. Once melted, fold in white frosting. When mixed you should have a light dough-like consistency.
3. Roll mixture into 1 inch balls and chill for 30 minutes.
4. Melt chocolate chips (highly recommend using Ghirardelli) in a double boiler. I use a rounded metal mixing bowl over a sauce pan with simmering water. Stir until smooth.
5. Place wax paper on a sheet pan and start dipping chilled peanut butter balls into chocolate using a toothpick. Keep a small circle of peanut butter showing around the toothpick.

6. After dipping, place each ball on the wax paper, leaving the toothpick intact.
7. Once the sheet is full, place in the fridge to chill.
8. Once set, remove the toothpicks and start eating.

Makes 2-3 dozen depending on how large or small you roll the peanut butter balls. Keep refrigerated as they will melt. Perfect for the holidays.

***

Terri Osburn writes contemporary romance with heart, hope, and lots of humor. After landing on the bestseller lists with her Anchor Island Series, she moved on to the Ardent Springs series, which earned her a Book Buyers Best award in 2016. Terri's work has been translated into five languages, and has sold more than 1.5 million copies worldwide. She resides in middle Tennessee with four frisky felines, and two high-maintenance terrier mixes.

Rum Balls
Nina Crespo

I was born and raised in the Southwest. My husband is from Puerto Rico. Including family favorites in our holiday meals has added a richness to our table, but we've also developed a few food traditions of our own. Rum Balls as a tradition happened by accident.

One year, while preparing our Christmas meal, I was running low on butter. My husband and I had to decide between having homemade dinner rolls or homemade cookies. We both voted to keep the rolls. But after glancing through different dessert recipes, I discovered I had the ingredients for Rum Balls. I made them and our own holiday food tradition as a couple began. You'll find them in our refrigerator on Christmas or New Year's Eve.

Ingredients
    1 cup crushed chocolate-filled wafer cookies (*This is a square, crisp cookie with chocolate filling not a round hard cookie. Visit a store that specializes in gourmet items or search the gourmet section at the store. Online buying is also an option. Examples: Loacker Quadratini® chocolate filled wafer cookies or Manner® Chocolate Cream-filled wafers.)
    ½ cup chopped walnuts or pecans
    1 cup powdered sugar
    2 tbsp unsweetened cocoa powder
    2 tbsp corn syrup
    ⅛ - ¼ cup rum (or brandy)
    *⅛ cup additional powdered sugar for rolling the finished cookies

Directions

1. Mix all ingredients in a bowl until well combined. It will be a wet, dough-like consistency. If the consistency is too loose, add in ¼ cup crushed wafers or 1-2 tbsp of cocoa.
2. Cover the bowl with plastic wrap or foil and refrigerate the mixture for four hours or overnight.
3. Form mixture into 1-inch round balls and roll in powdered sugar. Rum balls can be stored at room temperature for a softer texture or refrigerated for a fudge-like texture.

Preparation tips:

- Non-alcoholic substitutions for rum: apple cider or white grape juice or a combination of the two with a dash of almond extract.
- Use dark cocoa for richer flavor.
- Roll rum balls in a mixture of powdered sugar and cocoa or roll them in coconut flakes.

Yield: 1 ½ - 2 dozen

***

Nina Crespo lives in Florida where she indulges in her favorite passions – the beach, a good glass of wine, date night with her own real-life hero and dancing.

Her sensual contemporary stories satisfy a reader's craving for love, romance, and happily ever after.

Almond Biscotti (Tuscan Dipping Cookies)
A.S. Fenichel

Biscotti means "to bake twice". That's why traditional biscotti is so hard. I prefer to only bake it once, as it is still a firm cookie, but not tooth-breaking. But if you want to bake it again, turn each slice on its side and pop it back in the oven for ten minutes.

Also, feel free to add in some dried cranberries or drizzle with melted dark chocolate. Both are delicious additions. If you have a nut allergy you can skip the almonds and use vanilla extract, but then I highly recommend either cranberries or maybe orange zest to perk it up. Enjoy.

Lord help me, I love these cookies. This is another treat I learned to make on our honeymoon in Italy, and we love, love, love them. They are the perfect sweet. They take me back to Tuscany while making me feel at home at the same time.

Whenever we visit friends, I always bring a batch–along with the recipe–because I know they're going to want to make them after we leave. I love it when I get a message that someone made my biscotti and it turned out perfect. It's so nice to have those good friends think of me when they're enjoying a bit of my Italian experience.

I told you from the start that I show love through food. This biscotti is the ultimate sign of my friendship and love.

Some people knit to show their love. Others are quilt makers and will create beautiful creations to gift the people they love. I show my love through food. If you come to my house, I feed you. I feed you well and often. I may feed you too much, but I know you will love it. I will revel in your enjoyment of my food and look forward to the next time I can feed you.

With love, Andie.

What you need:
  ½ stick of butter
  1 cup of sugar
  2 large eggs
  1½ cups of flour
  ½ cup whole almonds
  1 tsp baking powder
  1 tsp almond extract

Directions
1. Preheat your oven to 350 Fahrenheit.
2. With your fingers, blend together butter and sugar. (The heat from your hands will melt them together and you can't get the right result with a spoon. Once it's well blended, you can wash your hands.)
3. With a spoon or rubber spatula, mix in the eggs.
4. Add the almonds and mix well before adding flour, baking powder, and almond extract.
5. Line a baking sheet with parchment paper and slid the dough into the middle. Use your hands to shape the dough into a flat loaf about 1 inch thick. TRICK: This is a sticky dough. Wet your hands to keep the dough from sticking to you as you shape it into the loaf.
6. Bake for 35-40 minutes until golden brown.
7. While the loaf is still warm, slice it about an inch thick and set aside to cool.

***

A.S. Fenichel (Andie) gave up a successful IT career to pursue her lifelong dream of being a professional writer. She is the author of more than twenty-five books full of love, passion, desire, magic, and maybe a little mayhem tossed in for good measure.

Anzac Slice
Penelope Janu

This recipe is a variation of the famous (in Australia and New Zealand!) Anzac Biscuit recipe. We traditionally eat these biscuits on ANZAC Day (25 April), the day that commemorates Australian and New Zealand military personnel who died during wartime. My daughter Tamsin Janu, a children's author (and a keen cook!) developed this variation on the biscuit.

Ingredients:
Rolled oats (traditional whole oats) – 1 cup
Self-rising flour – 1 cup
White sugar – 1 cup
Coconut – 1 cup
Walnuts – $\frac{1}{3}$ cup (sultanas can be used as an alternative)
Egg – 1
Butter (110 grams; 4 oz)
Vanilla essence – a few drops
Golden syrup (or honey) – 1 tablespoon

Process:
1. Mix the dry ingredients.
2. Melt the butter and golden syrup and add to dry ingredients.
3. Add egg and vanilla and mix well.
4. Spread mixture into a greased slice tray and press down firmly.
5. Cook in a slow oven (160 degrees Celsius; 320 Fahrenheit) for 30 – 40 minutes.
6. When cool, ice with lemon or orange icing (soft icing sugar, 1 tbs of lemon rind, and lemon juice, or 1 tbs of orange rind, and orange juice). Divide into squares.

Chapter Nine
Desserts

Mud
Beverly Jenkins

I make Mud for my family every Christmas, and I'd better not arrive at the gathering without it. In my book INDIGO our hero Galen teaches heroine Hester how to make mudpies, so this recipe is a play on that and is included in the book. I hope your family enjoys this yummy treat as much as my hero loves his heroine.

Cake
2c. sugar
1 c butter/margarine
4 eggs
1½ c flour
⅓ c cocoa
¼ t. salt
1 t vanilla
1 c nuts – chopped (optional)
½ pkg. 10oz marshmallows – (the little ones)

Icing
1- 1lb box confect sugar
1 t vanilla
1 c chopped nuts (optional)
1/3 c cocoa
1/3 c milk
1 c margarine - melted

Cake
1. Cream butter and sugar. Add eggs – mix well.
2. Sift together flour, cocoa, and salt – add to creamed mixture in increments. Mix well.
3. Add nuts and vanilla. Pour into greased 13x9 pan. 350 for 35 mins. Remove from oven and spread a layer of marshmallows over surface – (one layer deep).
4. ***Return to oven for additional 10 mins***. Cool.

Icing.
1. Sift sugar and cocoa into bowl, mix in melted butter.
2. Add milk and vanilla – then nuts.

Cake will be soft. Cover and let sit overnight.

Trifle
Lorraine Heath

My mother brought this recipe with her from England but "Americanized" it. The comments within parentheses and the PS are her words. She always served at Christmas.

Ingredients:
> Pound Cake slices or sponge cakes.
> Canned fruit of your choice (I use orange segments; others use fruit cocktail).
> Jello® flavor of choice
> Vanilla Jello® pudding
> Chocolate Jello® pudding

To make:
1. Soak cake in canned fruit and Jello® (made with fruit liquid & water – about ½ of liquid called for on Jello® box – also optional a dash of sherry or brandy (very English – very tasty).
2. Let set – make up Jello® puddings – cool slightly – pour onto cooled Jello®·cake·fruit mixture – to add to color effect layer the Jello® puddings.
3. Top with fresh whipped cream (just before serving), chopped nuts, and shredded chocolate can be sprinkled on top also.

PS. In England "Blanc Mange Mixtures" are used in place of the vanilla and chocolate pudding mixtures. I had to substitute here – they are somewhat the same thing but come in many different fruit flavors – might be found in British store or in Foreign Food section of grocery store; otherwise tint lightly part of vanilla pudding mixture with food color – preferably pink.

***

Lorraine Heath is the *New York Times* and *USA Today* bestselling author of western and Victorian-set historical romances. Born in England, she was raised in Texas and celebrates both her heritages in her stories.

Cream Puffs
Lorraine Heath

My mother brought this recipe over from England with her. It was a favorite served during holidays and large gatherings.

Ingredients:
- ½ C. Butter
- 4 Eggs
- 1 C. Boiling Water
- 1 C. Sifted Flour

Directions
1. Melt butter in boiling water.
2. Pour flour all at once into water and butter mixture, stirring constantly over low heat until mixture leaves sides of pan in smooth compact mass.
3. Remove from heat, beat in unbeaten eggs one at a time. Continue beating until mixture forms a thick dough.
4. Drop by tablespoons onto greased baking sheet, 1.5 inches apart, piling dough high.
5. Bake at 450 degrees for 20 minutes, then reduce temperature to 350 degrees for 20 minutes longer.
6. Remove from baking sheet and cool.
7. Open cream puff, pull out anything that hasn't baked crisply so you have only a shell remaining. Fill with whipped cream and top with chocolate sauce.

Nan's Pineapple Soufflé
Judi Fennell

This is my grandmother's recipe that I make for both Easter and Thanksgiving. At Easter, I serve it cold with ice cream, and at Thanksgiving, I serve it warm... with ice cream. What can I say? Ice cream goes with any holiday in my opinion...

My grandmother is gone now, but this recipe sets a place for her at our table every holiday. She was my first reader for my first book, *In Over Her Head*, a RomCom twist on *The Little Mermaid*, and thoroughly enjoyed the blog tours I did, using this recipe as a tie-in since... ya know, pineapples... tropical islands... mermaids...

So dive into the romance... and the soufflé!

Ingredients
1 C sugar
¼ lb butter
4 eggs
5 pieces bread, cubed
20 oz. crushed pineapple, drained

Directions
1. Pre-heat oven to 350. Grease 8" square pan.
2. Cream sugar and butter together.
3. Add eggs one at a time.
4. Put in greased pan.
5. Fold in crushed pineapple and bake about 45 minutes until knife in center comes out clean

Judi's Apple Pie
Judi Fennell

This recipe came into my life in my 7th grade Home Economics class. Our teacher taught us all to make crust from scratch and it's delicious! Apple pie has always been one of my favorite desserts so it was perfect when I learned to make it. I made it so often that I adapted the recipe to my particular taste and it became a family holiday staple all these years and my family calls it Judi's Apple Pie. In middle school, I entered a community pie-baking contest against a *lot* of apple pies. Including one my Home Ec teacher made.

Mine won and I've enjoyed baking ever since. Perhaps that's why I had one of my characters, Lara, become a baker in my book, *Beefcake & Cupcakes*, where Girls' Night Out never tasted so good!

Pre-heat oven to 375. Bake for 45 minutes.

Ingredients

Crust:
2 C flour, sifted
1 t salt
2/3 C + 2 T shortening
4-5 T ice water
Flour in reserve for rolling

Filling:
¾ C sugar
¼ C flour
½ t cinnamon
Dash salt
5 medium apples, peeled, cored, sliced thin.

Crust:
1. Mix flour and salt with a fork in a stainless-steel bowl (is best, but can use glass).
2. With a pastry blender (or fork), cut in shortening until mixture resembles small pebbles.

3. Add water in by Tablespoon, stiffing with a fork until the dough starts to clump together. Then bunch dough with hands to form a large ball. Halve the ball, the smaller ball for the bottom crust, the larger for the top.
4. Put in bowl and cover with a damp paper towel.

Filling:
1. Mix all dry ingredients in a new bowl.
2. Fold in apples gently, coating with sugar mixture.
3. Let sit for while rolling out crust.

To make pie:
1. Flour the surface and rolling pin.
2. Roll out bottom crust, occasionally using an offset spatula to make sure crust isn't stuck to surface. Re-flour as necessary. Check size by turning pie plate upside down and holding it over the rolled-out crust. The crust should extend 1-2" beyond the pie plate.
3. To pick up the crust, run the offset spatula under the entire crust, then use rolling pin to roll half the crust onto it and lift. Slide the pie plate under it and situate the crust in the plate.
4. Fold the apple/sugar mixture into the pie plate. (You can sprinkle extra cinnamon on top.)
5. Roll out the larger ball for the top crust in the same manner as the bottom and place over the top.
6. Crimp the edges all around.
7. Use a fork to poke 6 sets of vent holes around the top crust. Slice an 1" X in the middle with knife/offset spatula.
8. Bake for 45 minutes in 375-degree oven. Can broil for a minute or two to make the top crust browner if desired.

***

Judi Fennell, #1 Amazon and award-winning author, loves love and loves to laugh, so there's some in every book she writes. Check out her light-hearted, tongue-in-cheek paranormal and romantic comedies at www.JudiFennell.com. From mermen to genies, to men in maid's uniforms and male strippers, there's always a laugh and love to be had. In her spare(?) time, she helps authors with indie-publishing with her formatting, cover/promotional design, editorial, company, www.formatting4U.com. Judi's family includes many four-legged friends, and the minute those creatures start A) singing, B) sewing clothing, or C) cleaning the house will be the day she retires from writing...

Mevlyn's Pound Cake
Dee Davis

My grandmother's name was Mary Evelyn. But as a kid, I couldn't pronounce it and so called her Mevlyn, which soon became her name among family. This was her 'company' cake. And when she made it, she'd make a miniature version just for me.

Ingredients
   3 cups sugar
   1½ cups butter
   5 eggs
   3 cups flour
   1 tsp lemon, almond and vanilla extract
   1 cup milk

Directions
1. Cream butter and sugar and then beat in eggs one at a time.
2. Add flour alternating with milk and extracts.
3. Pour into tube or loaf pan.
4. Bake at 350° for 1 hr.

***

Bestselling author **Dee Davis** is the author of over thirty novels, including award winning time travel romance and romantic suspense. When not frantically trying to meet a deadline, Dee spends her time in her Connecticut farmhouse with her husband and Cardigan Welsh Corgis.

White Christmas
Penelope Janu

In Australia, we celebrate Christmas in summer, making this warm weather and easily prepared recipe a favourite with many 'down under' families. Notwithstanding the heat of the day, we often eat a traditional turkey and trimmings, with steamed plum pudding, but this accompaniment is a refreshing addition-or alternative-to traditional Christmas desserts. And as to the quantities-it is fine to adjust them as you wish.

Ingredients:
- 1 litre (4½ cups) of frozen yoghurt (wildberry or berry swirl, or any fruity frozen yoghurt). Fruit sorbet, or a fruity ice cream, are alternatives.
- 1 litre (4½ cups) vanilla ice cream
- Pavlova case (a store-purchased crunchy meringue case is ideal). Crumble this meringue to 2 cups of crunchiness.
- Frozen mixed berries – 3 to 4 cups

Process:
1. Spoon half the berry yogurt into a bowl.
2. On top of it, layer a quarter of the berries. Then layer half the vanilla ice cream, and sprinkle with meringue. Layer half the berries and pack down. Layer the remaining berry yoghurt, and the remaining vanilla ice cream.
3. Sprinkle with remaining berries. Cover and freeze.
4. I prepare this dessert in a large crystal bowl (a wedding present). The layers look fabulous!

Defrost for fifteen minutes before serving.

Grandma Loveland's Graham Cracker Pie
JoAnn Brown

When I was growing up, Thanksgiving meant turkey and all the fixings as well as green bean casserole, cranberry sauce... and Grandma's pies. She made lemon meringue for my sisters and graham cracker for me. We celebrated each Thanksgiving with my mother's parents and her brother. We kids loved slipping into the kitchen where barely controlled chaos reigned among the most delicious aromas. Then, one year, we woke on Thanksgiving to almost three feet of snow. My grandparents and uncle lived about ten miles away. Twice my dad tried to get out to the main road in order to pick them up and bring them to join us. The second time he got to the main road, but it hadn't been plowed, so he had to turn around and come home. We had our Thanksgiving dinner without them. It simply wasn't the same. We missed having them with us, and we missed the pinnacle of the meal – Grandma's pies. Every year since then (except for one year when I didn't have an oven), I've made a graham cracker pie. Our family had a five generation get-together for Thanksgiving a couple of years ago, and the call at the end of the meal was, "Where's the graham cracker pie?" Fortunately, I'd made three, so there was enough for everyone to have piece along with the other types of pie. It's a family tradition that's easy to make and delicious to eat!

Ingredients for 9" pie:
Crust:
     1½ cups of crushed graham crackers
     1 stick of butter/margarine
     ⅓ cup of sugar

1. Melt the butter in the microwave. Using a fork, combine melted butter with graham crackers and sugar. Make sure you get all crackers mixed in with the butter. Pour out all but a tablespoon into a pie pan. Press into place.
2. Bake at 400 degrees for 8 minutes or until golden brown.

Filling:

    2 packages of vanilla pudding (3.4 oz size)

    4 cups of milk (I use whole milk to give it the creamiest flavor. 2% works as well. NOTE: Milk alternatives may not work with packaged pudding)

1. Prepare according to instructions on the box. It doesn't matter if you choose instant or cooked pudding.
2. Pour pudding into pie shell and put into the refrigerator. It can sit overnight, but is better if you make it the day you're going to serve it.

Meringue:

    3 eggs, whites only

    6 tablespoons of sugar

    ½ teaspoon of vanilla

1. Separate the eggs (I save the yolks for my cats as a treat) and put egg whites in a mixing bowl
2. Set your mixer at its highest speed and beat egg whites.
3. When they begin to foam, add a single teaspoon of sugar. Once that is beaten in, repeat for all six tablespoons. Do NOT add them all at once because it will take a very long time to get the meringue to the proper consistency.
4. Beat until the meringue stands in place when you stop the mixer and pull it out.
5. Add vanilla and beat a minute longer.
6. Spoon onto the pie and swirl to make a pretty pattern. Cook at 400 degrees for 8-10 minutes (until golden brown)
7. Cool... and enjoy!

***

JoAnn Brown has published over 100 titles under a variety of pen names since selling her 1st book in 1987. A former military officer, she enjoys telling stories, taking pictures, and traveling. She has taught creative writing for more than 20 years and is always excited when one of her students sells a project. She has been married for more than 30 years and has three children. Currently she lives in Nevada

Cream Cheese Pound Cake
Tracey Livesay

I didn't grow up baking but once I had kids, it became a skill I quickly learned. When I was ready to graduate from store mixes to homemade goodies, I consulted my grandmother, the best cook I knew. This is the first cake I ever attempted on my own. Let's say, over the years, the end result got better. ☺ While delicious on its own, I usually serve it as the base of strawberry shortcake. I'll cut up strawberries, macerate them with sugar (and a little champagne for the adults) and then top the cake with the strawberries, chocolate syrup and whipped cream. It's absolute heaven. Enjoy!

Ingredients
> 1 (8 oz) package cream cheese
> 1¼ cups butter, softened
> 3½ cups white sugar
> 7 eggs, yolks & whites divided
> 2 tsp butter-flavored extract
> 2 2/3 cups all-purpose flour
> ¼ tsp salt
> ¼ tsp baking powder

Directions
1. Preheat oven to 350 degrees F. Grease and flour a 10 inch bundt pan. Sift together the flour, salt and baking powder. Set aside.
2. In a large bowl, cream butter, cream cheese, and sugar until light and fluffy. Beat in egg yolks one at a time. Beat in the butter flavoring. Beat in the flour mixture.

3. In a large glass or metal mixing bowl, beat egg whites until stiff peaks form. Fold 1/3 of the whites into the batter, then quickly fold in remaining whites until no streaks remain. Pour into greased and floured bundt pan.
4. Bake at 350 degrees F for about an hour, or until toothpick comes out clean.

12 Servings | Prep Time: 30 minutes| Total Time: 1 hr, 30 min

Maine Blackberry Cobbler
Belle Calhoune

A recipe my mother used to make for us when I was growing up. We spent a summer vacation in Maine (my parents and 5 kids) and we stayed at an inn where they served amazing meals in a large dining room. One of the most delicious treats we tasted was hot out of the oven blackberry cobbler. Once we got home my mom did her best to recreate it, with delicious results.

Ingredients:
   2½ cups fresh Blackberries (washed and patted dry)
   1 tsp of Lemon
   1 tsp of nutmeg
   1 cup of sugar (divided in half)
   1 cup of milk
   1 cup of flour
   2 teaspoons baking power
   ½ teaspoon salt
   ½ cup butter (melted)

Directions
1. Lightly grease a 9 by 13 baking dish (or any comparable size).
2. Take a tsp of lemon juice and pour over washed blackberries.
3. Then add one half cup of the sugar and 1 tsp

of nutmeg. The sugar will draw out the juices in the blackberries.

4. In another bowl mix the remaining ingredients… there will only be ½ cup of sugar left.
5. Once you have mixed these ingredients thoroughly, pour into baking dish.
6. Then fold the blackberry mix into dish.
7. Bake at 350 for 40 minutes.

Can be garnished with whipped cream and served with vanilla ice cream.

*Best with fresh blackberries.

Cottage Cheese Pie
Linda Warren

In her later years my grandmother came to live with us, and she brought her cow. Now that could have been a problem had we lived in the city, but we lived in rural Texas so Bessie was welcome. My grandmother milked her every day and we had fresh butter, cream, buttermilk and cottage cheese. She didn't like the milk products my mother bought at the store. One of the things she made during the holidays was cottage cheese pie. It's like a custard or chess. I can remember her making it and how delicious it was with all the fresh ingredients. After she passed away, my mother would make it during holidays. My mother passed 20 years ago without one word written down how to make it. I've been doing my best to duplicate that recipe ever since and when I do, I think of the holidays, family and love. Momma and Grandma, I hope I've done you proud.

Ingredients
3 Eggs
¾ cup sugar
16 oz of Cottage cheese
1 tsp vanilla
½ cup cream (I started out using half and half and then tried evaporated milk for less calories)
¼ tsp Cinnamon
Pie crust

Directions:
1. Beat eggs and sugar together.
2. Add next ingredients and mix together.

3. Pour into a deep dish pie crust. It makes a big pie.
4. Bake 350° for 45 minutes or until it doesn't jiggle.

You'll love it!

Mocha Oatmeal Cake
Casey Hagen

This is the cake of all cakes guys. Chocolate lovers adore this cake. People who complain when desserts are too chocolatey, they love it too! Those coffee haters? They have no clue coffee is even in it. It's down home and fancy all in one... good for literally any occasion. And, great news! You can slice it into servings, wrap it in plastic wrap, and store it in the fridge for up to two weeks. Bad news if you live alone, made it for yourself, and want to use the excuse that you just had to snarf it down in three days or it would go to waste.

My dad adored this cake... and when I married my husband, I brought it to my father-in-law who fell in love with it too! I even made it for him this last Christmas and shipped it to them. It ships beautifully!

Ingredients:
1 tbsp. instant coffee
1½ cups boiling water
(If you don't have the above, you can use 1-1/2 cups of fresh brewed coffee)
1 cup quick oats
¾ cup butter
1 cup brown sugar
2 eggs
2 cups flour
3 tbsp. cocoa
1½ tsp. vanilla
1½ tsp. baking soda

Directions:
1. Combine coffee, oatmeal, water, butter, and sugar.
2. Cool 20 minutes.
3. Add beaten eggs and vanilla.
4. Blend in dry ingredients.
5. Bake in a greased and floured tube pan at 350 degrees for 50-55 minutes.
6. Transfer to cooling rack after about five minutes.

Frosting
1 tbsp. milk
1½ tbsp. soft or melted butter
1 cup confectionary sugar

Blend and drizzle over the cake fresh out of the pan while it's still hot. It will soak in some. It will slide down the sides and make a mess.

It will be freaking amazing!

Chocolate Town Special Cake
Nikki Brock

This recipe was clipped from a small-town Kentucky newspaper in the Forties. My grandmother made it for everyone's birthday, as did my mother, and now I make it.

Ingredients:
1¾ c. sugar
⅔ c. butter or shortening, softened
2 eggs
1 tsp. vanilla extract
2½ c cake flour, sifted
1½ tsp. baking soda
½ tsp. salt
1 c. buttermilk
½ c. cocoa powder
½ c. boiling water

Directions:
1. Preheat oven to 350 degrees (325 degrees if using dark cake pans).
2. Grease and flour 2 9-inch cake pans.
3. Beat shortening and sugar together until light and fluffy. Add eggs, one at a time, beating well after each addition. Add vanilla.
4. Sift together flour, baking soda, and salt. Add alternately with the buttermilk to the shortening-sugar mixture.
5. Make a heavy paste of cocoa powder and boiling water; let cool, then add and blend well.
6. Pour into prepared cake pans; bake for about 25 minutes or until cake tester comes out clean.
7. Cool and frost with Creamy Chocolate Under-Frosting.

Creamy Chocolate Under–Frosting
Nikki Brock

Don't let the raw egg in the frosting spook you; in eighty years of cake-making, no one has gotten sick yet.

Ingredients:
½ c. butter, softened
⅛ tsp. salt
1 lb. (about 1 box) unsifted confectioner's sugar
8 squares Baker's unsweetened chocolate, melted and cooled
1 egg
1 tsp. vanilla extract
¼ c. milk

Directions:
1. Cream butter until soft. Beat in the salt and about 1 ½ cups of the sugar.
2. Add egg, vanilla and melted chocolate; blend well.
3. Beat in remaining sugar alternately with the milk, beating well after each addition until smooth. (If necessary, place bowl of frosting in larger bowl of cold water and chill until frosting is of spreading consistency.)
4. Use to fill and frost 2 or 3 cake layers.

Chocolate Zucchini Cake
Lucy Farago

I love cooking. I find it most useful when my muse needs a good kick in the pants. Creativity spurs creativity, didn't you know. I also enjoy sharing what I cook. During the worst of the pandemic, when there wasn't much else to do, when morale was at its lowest and uncertainty at its highest, I baked... and then shared. Food, after all, brings comfort.

I learned the art of sourdough bread, friendship cake and using an abundance of the zucchini my husband planted. *He* learned how to plant a garden. My Instagram is full of food pics. My neighbors were happy–me, I... er... gained several pounds.

On the plus side, I released another book, and I caught up on my glorious 'to be read' pile...while eating everything I'd learned to cook. Oh well, my neighbors loved me, and my dog, he got three walks a day.

1. Grate 4 cups zucchini. Then gently hand-squeeze the water out, in order to make 3 cups. Put aside.
2. Wire-whisk... then set aside...
   2 cups all-purpose flower
   ¼ cup cocoa powder, unsweetened (if you want more chocolate, add ½ cup)
   2 tsp baking soda
   1 tsp baking powder
   ½ tsp salt
   1 tsp cinnamon
   ½ tsp all spice (you can substitute nutmeg)

3. Mix...
   - ¾ cup vegetable oil
   - ¼ cup melted, cooled butter (brown butter if you have it)
   - ½ cup white sugar (I use vanilla sugar...see below)
   - ¾ cup brown sugar (not packed)
   - 3 large eggs
   - ¼ cup Greek yogurt (you can substitute sour cream)
   - 1 tsp vanilla
4. Beat until thoroughly combined.
5. Blend in zucchini, and if you wish... ½ cup semi-sweet chocolate chips and/or ½ cup chopped walnuts.
6. Stir in flour mixture only until incorporated.

This will make two 9" round cakes or 24 muffins.

Bake 350F 25-30 minutes for cake pans. 20 minutes for muffins. Done when toothpick comes out clean.

This cake can be frosted with chocolate, vanilla or cream cheese frosting or it's delicious by itself.

Vanilla Sugar
Lucy Farago

Ingredients
> 2 cups of sugar
> 1 vanilla bean

Option 1 (easy)
1. Cut 1 inch off a vanilla bean and toss in a mason jar with the sugar.
2. Shake the jar daily for 1 week.

You end up with a lovely scented sugar.

Option 2
1. Cut bean length wise.
2. Scrape the inside with a paring knife, removing the seeds. Then them toss in a food processor with the sugar and blend.
   You'll create a finer sugar, good for cooking, and will have dispersed the seeds. This can be done by hand as well.
3. Place the sugar in a glass jar with a tight lid, place the scraped bean inside the jar with the sugar.
   You'll end up with a more intense vanilla flavor.
   If you want, you could double the recipe and use the entire bean... or store the remainder in a sealed jar for another use.

Hint
Don't throw out the vanilla pod when you've used up all the sugar. It can be used again.

Better Than Birthday Cake–
AKA Better Than Sex Cake
Mindy Neff

I'm not sure where this recipe originated, but it's been a favorite dessert in our household for over forty years. When the grandkids came along, they began to request it as their birthday cake for their parties. Well, we ran into a bit of a problem when a bunch of seven-year-olds were winking and giggling with their little pals about Nana's Better Than Sex Cake, so we wisely renamed it to Better Than Birthday Cake.

Ingredients
   --Chocolate cake mix (boxed)
   --Eagle Brand Condensed milk (1 can)
   --Hershey's chocolate syrup (1 can)
   --Carmel syrup (1 can–can get this in a squeeze bottle also)
   --Heath bar or crumbled toffee candy
   --8 oz container of cool whip (can use larger carton if you like lots of cool whip like I do!)

Directions
1. Prepare cake mix per boxed instructions.
2. Pour into 9 x 13 pan. Bake according to boxed instructions. Let cake cool.
3. Poke holes all over top of cake with the round handle of a wooden spoon.
4. Pour sweetened condensed milk over the top and let it sink in.
5. Then pour chocolate syrup and caramel syrup over the top.
6. Spread with cool whipped topping and sprinkle with crushed heath bar or crumbled toffee candy.
7. Refrigerate and enjoy!

Perfect Chocolate Cake
Nikki Sloane

There's a restaurant in Chicago (my hometown) that's known for its hot dogs, Italian beef... and chocolate cake! The secret ingredient is the mayo, which creates a rich and moist cake. If I'm feeling homesick, a slice of this usually cures it.

Cake
> 2 cups flour
> ½ cup cocoa powder
> 1¼ tsp. baking soda
> ½ tsp. baking powder
> 1 tsp. instant coffee
> 1 pinch of salt
> 3 eggs, room temperature
> 1 cup real mayonnaise
> 1 cup sugar
> 1¼ cup water, ice cold
> 1 tsp. vanilla

Frosting
> 1 cup butter, softened
> ½ cup cocoa powder
> 5 cups powdered sugar
> 1 tsp. vanilla
> 3 Tbsp. milk (if needed)

Directions:

Cake
1. Preheat the oven to 350F.
2. Coat 2 round cake pans with non-stick spray and line with parchment paper.
3. Mix flour, cocoa powder, baking soda, baking powder, coffee, sugar, and salt in a bowl. Set aside.
4. Add the eggs, mayonnaise, water and vanilla into the dry ingredients. Mix until thoroughly combined, approximately two minutes. Divide the batter between the two prepared pans.
5. Bake for 22-28 minutes or until a toothpick inserted in the center comes out clean.
6. Cool the cakes completely before frosting.

Frosting
1. Cream butter, cocoa, and sugar together until smooth in large bowl.
2. Stir in vanilla.
3. Add milk one tablespoon at a time until frosting reaches desired consistency.
4. Whip until light, fluffy and smooth, 1-2 minutes.

Harvest Pie

Gemma Brocato

When I was a young teen, I loved to bake, but always seemed to add baking soda when baking powder was called for. One day, my cake came out looking like a volcano! He scribbled Gemma's Disaster in the powdered sugar on the slopes.

In my thirties, I entered a baking contest with this recipe, and when I won first prize, I sent a message to my bro that basically said – Take That!

Ingredients

Pastry for a 9" two crust pie (I cheat and use prepackaged crusts. I also go with a deep dish)

¾ cup brown sugar (packed)

¼ cup white sugar

⅓ cup flour

1 teaspoon cinnamon

¼ teaspoon nutmeg

4 cups sliced tart apples, peeled

2 cups cranberries (whole or chopped – reduced sugar Craisins work as well)

⅓ cup raisins (could omit is you don't like raisins)

1 orange peel, grated

1 jigger of almond liqueur (like Amaretto) More is okay

½ cup sliced almonds

Directions

1. In a large bowl, combine sugars, flour, cinnamon, and nutmeg.
2. Toss fruit and orange peel with the almond liqueur, then coat with the sugar mixture.
3. Sprinkle sliced almond on the bottom crust, the add the fruit mixture.
4. Dot with the butter, then cover with the top crust and trim and seal the edges.
5. If you want to do an egg wash on the top and sprinkle cinnamon-sugar, go for it. It will make the pie pretty.
6. Bake for 40 minutes at 425 degrees.

Brownies
Valerie Clarizio

This recipe came from my mother who passed away 30 years ago. It's still a favorite for my brothers and me. The smell of and taste of these delicious brownies unleashes warm family memories.

Ingredients
⅓ C Butter
⅓ C Cocoa
1 C Sugar
½ C Flour
2 Eggs
1 tsp Vanilla
½ tsp Baking Powder
½ tsp Salt

Directions
1. Combine melted butter and sugar. Stir in eggs and vanilla.
2. Beat in cocoa, flour, salt, and baking powder.
3. Spread batter into a greased, 9-inch square pan.
4. Bake at 350 degrees for 25-30 minutes.

Seeing as I have not yet found a homemade chocolate frosting that I like as much as Pillsbury Chocolate Fudge frosting, I cheat and top my homemade brownies with Pillsbury frosting.

Berries with Cream
Susan Wisnewski

Ingredients
½ pint Blueberries whole
½ pint strawberries halved or quartered if large
1 TBS Grand Marnier or other Liqueur (optional)
2 cans Real Whipped Cream (I like Cabot's)

Directions
1. If using the Grand Marnier or other fruity liqueur, toss berries with the liqueur.
2. Arrange berries in two wine glasses.
3. Top with whipped cream and serve.

I'm sure you know what to do with the second can of whipped cream! You're welcome.

***

Susan Peterson Wisnewski writes Romantic Suspense, Mystery and Paranormal novels. Her four novels, with more coming soon, challenge strong female characters to solve page turning mysteries with the help of hunky men.

Nisha's Slow Cooker Kheer
Nisha Sharma

Prep Time: 5 Minutes
Cook Time: 6 Hours

I was the weird kid that loved rice pudding, but in my defense, my mother's kheer was not the typical rice pudding that is sold in American grocery stores. It's best served warm, and flavored with raisons and cardamom. The past part about this recipe is that it is the perfect dessert to eat during late night reading. If it goes cold, it's still delicious!

Ingredients:
- ½ cup Basmati rice (can substitute Jasmine)
- 6 cups whole milk
- 8oz sweetened condensed milk
- 1 teaspoon cardamom powder
- ½ cup of peeled slivered almonds or roughly chopped pistachios (optional)
- ½ cup golden raisins (optional)

Instructions:
1. All you have to do is dump everything into a slow cooker for 6 hours on low heat.
2. Stir every hour. The first three hours it will be straight liquid but then it comes together pretty nicely. If it's way too thick, then you can add more liquid to it (whole milk), a quarter cup at a time, until it has a smooth, creamy texture.

3. Add raisins and almonds in at the last 1 hour mark, but that's totally optional.

You can also put little cut up pieces of chocolate at the end in there, and it tastes just as delicious.

And there you have it! The easy-peasy slow cooker method of making some kheer.

***

Nisha Sharma is the author of the critically acclaimed YA novel *My So-Called Bollywood Life* and the follow up, *Radha and Jai's Recipe for Romance*. She also writes adult contemporary romances including The Singh Family Trilogy and If Shakespeare was an Aunty Trilogy (Launching January 2022). Her writing has been praised by NPR, *Cosmopolitan* Magazine, *Teen Vogue*, Buzzfeed, Hypable and more.

Nisha credits her father for her multiple graduate degrees, and her mother for her love of Shah Rukh Khan and Jane Austen. She lives in Pennsylvania with her Alaskan husband, her cat Lizzie Bennett and her dog Nancey Drew.

Pumpkin Roll
Stephanie J. Scott

My grandma's pumpkin roll is another family favorite. My mom would triple the recipe and freeze the batches prior to the holidays and take them everywhere.

Ingredients
⅔ cup canned pumpkin
3 eggs
¾ cup flour
1 cup sugar
1 tsp salt
1 tsp baking soda
½ tsp cinnamon (truth: I use 1 full tsp!)
Powdered sugar to use post-bake

Filling:
8 oz cream cheese (can use 1/3 fat type/ Neufchatel cheese)
1 cup powdered sugar
2 Tbl butter
1 tsp vanilla (maple flavoring is a fun one to substitute!)

Directions
1. Set oven to 375 degrees. Mix eggs and sugar in a bowl.
2. Add in canned pumpkin and mix well.
3. Separately, add dry ingredients together and add into the wet mix.
4. Grease, or line with wax paper, a jelly roll pan (cookie sheet with sides) and pour in the batter.
5. Bake for 10 – 12 minutes.

Desserts

6. Remove from pan onto a clean dish towel covered with powdered sugar to prevent sticking (remove wax paper if used).
7. Roll up while still warm and cool/chill for 1 hour.
8. When cooled, unroll and spread the filling across one side the roll.
9. Roll back up and chill or freeze until ready to serve.
10. Take out 10 minutes before service to slice into individual discs.

***

Stephanie J. Scott writes young adult and romance about characters who put their passions first. Her debut ALTERATIONS about a fashion-obsessed loner who reinvents herself was a Romance Writers of America RITA® award finalist. She enjoys dance fitness, everything cats, and has a slight obsession with Instagram. A Midwest girl at heart, she resides outside of Chicago with her tech-of-all-trades husband and fuzzy furbabies.

Pistachio Cake
Jennifer Bray-Weber

I'm just a girl from Texas. And like most Southern girls, I love dessert. Especially decadent ones. One of my favorites is a vintage recipe once found on many Southern tables–Pistachio Cake, also known as Watergate Cake. Why is it called Watergate Cake? The story goes the name is a tongue-in-cheek reference to the political scandal of the 70s that rocked the United States. The icing "covers up" any imperfections and the cake is full of nuts. Drama and nuts aside, this dessert is easy to make and oh-so yummy!

Ingredients
Cake:
1 box white cake mix
1 package (3.5 oz.) instant pistachio pudding mix
3 eggs
1 cup vegetable oil
1 can (12 oz.) lemon-lime soda (such as Sprite or 7Up)
Frosting:
1 package (3.5 oz.) instant pistachio pudding mix
1 ½ cups milk
1 tub frozen whipped topping (8oz.), thawed
¼ cup chopped pistachio nuts, for garnish
Maraschino cherries, for garnish (optional)

Directions
Cake:
1. Heat oven to 350°. Coat two 9-inch round cake pans

273

with nonstick cooking spray. Line the bottoms of pans with wax paper and spray again.
2. Beat cake mix, pudding mix, eggs, vegetable oil, and soda on high for 2 minutes.
3. Divide batter equally into the pans. Bake for 35 minutes, or until an inserted toothpick comes out clean.
4. Cool completely before frosting

Frosting:
1. Beat pudding mix and milk until blended, about 2 minutes.
2. Fold in whipped topping
3. Place 1 cake layer on a serving plate and frost the top using about 1 cup of frosting. Place the remaining layer on top and frost the top and sides. Garnish with nuts and cherries (optional).
4. Refrigerate 1 hour before serving.

Pa's Kuchen
Tracey Devlyn

This recipe has been in my husband's family for generations. We make a batch of kuchen every Christmas. It's delicious and a big hit with the family. A few years ago, my Doberman decided that he wanted to sample the amazing scent emanating from the kitchen counter and he pulled the entire log off. He ate the WHOLE thing. All he left behind was tiny aluminum foil crumbs for us to find.

NOTE: Contains walnuts

DOUGH PREP
> 4 cups all-purpose flour
> ½ pound butter
> 2 tablespoon sugar
> 2 egg yolks (keep egg whites for later)
> 2 ounces of active dry yeast
> 1 scant cup of warm water (slightly less than one cup!)

Directions
1. Add yeast to warm water and let it stand while cutting butter into the flour until the mixture is coarse.
2. Add unbeaten yolks and yeast mixture. Mix together until dough leaves sides of bowl (~5 min).
3. Divide into 4 balls.
4. Let dough rest (resting softens the dough) while preparing nut filling.
5. Preheat oven to 400°F.

NUT FILLING
   1 pound walnuts
   ½ cup milk
   1 teaspoon vanilla
   1 cup sugar (to taste)

Directions
1. Heat milk, then add walnuts. Stir until milk is absorbed.
2. Remove from heat.
3. Add sugar and vanilla.

PUT IT ALL TOGETHER
1. Roll one dough ball into a rectangle.
2. Spread filling over the dough, evenly.
3. Roll it up, jelly-roll style.
4. Brush slightly beaten egg whites on top of the roll.
5. Line a cookie sheet with parchment paper and then place the roll on the cookie sheet.
6. Bake 10-15 minutes.
7. Let stand for 20 minutes. Repeat for the remaining 3 balls.
8. Cut the roll into one-inch pieces and enjoy!

Kuchen does great in the freezer. Freeze a few loaves and enjoy this tasty treat throughout the year!

Fabulous Fudge
Leslie Hachtel

I make this for Christmas gifts. It's labor intensive, but the compliments are worth it!

Ingredients:
   1⅓ cups granulated white sugar
   1 (7oz) jar of marshmallow crème
   ⅔ cup evaporated milk
   ¼ cup butter
   ¼ cup chocolate liqueur (like Mozart, Godiva or Kahlua)
   ¼ tsp. salt
   2 cups semi-sweet chocolate chips
   1 cup milk chocolate chips
   1 tsp. vanilla
   ⅔ cup chopped nuts (walnuts or pecans) (optional)

Directions
1. Line a 9x13 pan with waxed paper or tin foil. In large, deep saucepan combine sugar, marshmallow crème, milk, butter, liqueur, and salt.
2. Bring to a rapid boil.
3. Now – this is the most important part. Stir constantly for five full minutes (any less and the fudge will not set).
4. Remove from heat and stir in chocolate chops until melted. Add vanilla and nuts.
5. Pour into 9x13 pan and refrigerate until firm (about 4 hours). Peel off waxed paper or foil and cut into small squares. (It's super rich!)

The Best Chocolate Cake...
Lisa Kessler

Lisa Kessler's Recipe hacks to make you look like you can bake!

I write paranormal romances, but sadly that magic has never carried over into the kitchen for me. In fact, I've caught myself on fire twice in that scary room! Over the years I've learned to compensate with some terrific cooking hacks that can make you look like an expert, even if you're secretly using a box mix like me.

Anyone can make cake with a box of mix, but everyone will think you made this moist rich cake from scratch with this hack.

Grab your boxed cake mix and follow the recipe until you get to the eggs. You're going to use 4 eggs and add 1 box of chocolate pudding mix to the batter (not instant pudding). Bake as instructed on the box.

Your cake will be fluffy and moist, and no one will believe you didn't make it from scratch.

Another hack for the frosting. If you're making a Bundt cake, you can artistically drizzle the chocolate frosting over the cake without making it from scratch. Start with a plastic tub of frosting and remove the lid and foil. Put a square of wax paper over the top and put it in the microwave for 45 – 60 seconds. Take it out and stir the frosting. It should be a thick liquid texture. You can either slowly pour the frosting onto the cake from the tub, or use the spoon if you just want a little drizzle.

THE MOST AWESOME CHOCOLATE FUDGE CAKE EVER
Nancy C. Weeks

I received this recipe from my sweet mother-in-law at my bridal shower in a Heritage Cookbook, and it was labeled Jill Baker's cake. She had hand written all of my hubby's favorite recipes and had asked my mother to do the same thing. Since chocolate cake and chocolate frosting were my favorite since childhood, I made this recipe in our new home as soon as our kitchen was unpacked. I quickly renamed the recipe *The Most Awesome Chocolate Fudge Cake Ever!* Over the last forty years, I've made this cake hundreds of times. It's one of those recipes you just dump everything in the bowl, mix, and if you're careful not to burn it, it comes out amazing every time. It's my kids favorite for every occasion. I have frozen the batter in freezer storage bags, let it defrost on the counter, and we have cake whenever we want it. I have made the cake, frosted it, placed it in the freezer overnight, and shipped it across the country. It arrives in perfect shape, time and again. I wish I could thank Jill for her incredible gift that has brought such joy to so many people. I hope it has the same effect on those you love. Enjoy!

Ingredients
    2 C sugar
    ½ C butter (one stick)
    2 eggs
    1 tsp vanilla
    ½ tsp almond extract - optional
    1 C milk–I use 2%

½ C cocoa powder or 4 squares of unsweetened chocolate
2½ C flour
1 tsp. Baking powder
1 tsp baking soda
1 C water-almost at a boil

Directions
1. Melt chocolate in microwave for 1 minute. No need if you use cocoa powder.
2. In a mixing bowl, mix butter, sugar, eggs, and vanilla.
3. Add chocolate slowly.
4. Add flour, baking soda, baking powder, alternating with milk.
5. Mix well for about 2 minutes.
6. Slowly add the super-hot water, almost boiling. Mix until well blended.
7. Pour into a buttered 13x9-inch baking pan, 2 round cake pans or 24 cupcakes.
8. Bake at 350F for 30 minutes.
9. Cool before frosting if you have time. It is wonderful warm, too.

THE MOST AWESOME FUDGE CHOCOLATE ICING
Nancy C. Weeks

It takes all of 5 minutes. Make extra for the cook and find a great hiding place in the refrigerator.

Bring to a soft boil:
>   1 stick of butter
>   4 Tbs. cocoa or 2 squares of unsweetened chocolate
>   ¼ C of milk
>   1 Tsp vanilla

Directions
1. Pour over 1 pound of powdered sugar.
2. Beat well.
3. Add more milk a tablespoon at a time if needed. It looks strange at first, but after you beat it well, it will smooth out. I use my wire whip for making whip cream. It makes it super creamy.

Mix Things Up
Add to the frosting once creamy...
>   Coconut
>   Pecans–Nuts of any kind
>   Broken pieces of any type of candy
>   Toffee
>   Chocolate covered coffee beans
>   Chocolate covered anything...

Think about your favorite fudge and then just go to town... And yes, bacon... it's delicious!

Strawberry Pie
Beth Carter

My dad, who loves pie more than any other dessert, said this pie is divine. I agree! It's perfect for spring and summer and makes a beautiful presentation.

Ingredients
1 cup sugar (may use Splenda blend)
1 cup water
½ package wild strawberry Jell-O
1 heaping T. cornstarch
1 quart fresh sliced strawberries, sliced
1 9-inch pie shell, baked

Directions
1. Bake pie shell according to package directions. Allow to cool.
2. Combine sugar, cornstarch, and water in a small saucepan. Cook over low heat until thickened and beginning to clear.
3. Remove from heat and add Jell-O. Stir and set aside until completely cool.
4. Combine liquid with strawberries and pour into baked pie shell.
5. Refrigerate several hours or overnight until set. I always double the recipe for family gatherings.

Optional: Top slices with Cool Whip or vanilla ice cream.

Serves: 8 (unless you eat like my husband!)

The Cake of a Thousand Faces
Susan Wiggs

This is my standby cake from a recipe that probably originated in Sunset Magazine and was passed along to me by friend, fellow author, and bookshop owner Suzanne Selfors. It gets its name because it's so versatile. You can use almost any fruit, nuts, or just butter to make a fiendishly seductive cake. I almost always have the ingredients on hand and I can get creative, adding favorite flavors, using seasonal ingredients, even turning it into a holiday masterpiece. There's no way to mess up this cake.

Ingredients
    1 stick softened butter (never margarine)
    1 cup flour
    1 cup sugar
    1 teaspoon baking powder
    2 large eggs
    A pinch of salt

Directions
1. Beat all the ingredients together until smooth. Spread the thick batter into a buttered tart pan or springform pan.
2. Now add what you want. For instance, use about a cup of blackberries, pressed into the top of the tart.

For a pear theme, thinly slice ripe pears and arrange in a pinwheel pattern. I've had success with raspberries, blueberries, plum, and peach. Almond flavoring and sliced almonds are good, too.
3. Bake at 350 degrees. Depending on the size of your tart pan, it can take anywhere from 45 to 55 minutes.

Make a glaze of apricot jam and a squeeze of lemon melted together. Brush with the glaze, then dust with powdered sugar if you'd like, and serve with whipped cream, crème fraiche, or ice cream.

Darlene's Lazy Daisy Cake
Jo McNally

My 95-year-old mom is in hospice care as I write this, but she's been a strong-willed, globetrotting fashionista right up until the past few months. In fact, just over a year ago she was still hopping on planes alone and flying off to visit family and friends. She was in her 80s when she announced she was going to China, quickly followed by a European river cruise with her sister, and then a tour of Ireland. She is always in style, too, no matter what the occasion.

Mom and her equally independent sister, Shirley, were a major inspiration for the sassy, funny, wise women in the matchmaking bookclub of my contemporary romance series, Rendezvous Falls. I often say that not ALL grandmas in romance novels have to wear ruffled aprons and bake cookies. But the truth is, my mom--raised on an Iowa farm--was both a modern working woman AND an excellent cook, among other things. I come from good stock!

And this recipe? This was her signature cake. It's so good that my brother, my dad and I usually asked for it for our birthdays, even though sticking candles in it is almost impossible. And it goes so fast that you'll probably want to double it. Seriously. It's *that* good. And relatively easy, other than keeping a close eye on the topping while broiling.

285

Cake Ingredients:
½ stick butter or margarine
½ cup whole milk
1 tsp. vanilla
¼ tsp. salt
1 cup sugar
1 cup flour
1 tsp baking powder
2 eggs

Topping Ingredients:
½ stick butter or margarine
¾ cup brown sugar
5 Tbsp cream
⅔ cup combo of coconut and chopped pecans/walnuts
(you can do all coconut, too)

Directions

Cake:
1. In small sauce pan, heat the butter and the milk (not too hot--don't scald it).
2. Add vanilla.
3. Beat eggs and sugar and cream well.
4. Add dry ingredients alternately with the milk mixture.
5. Pour in lightly greased and floured 9x9 pan and bake at 350° for 20 minutes.

Topping:
1. Melt butter and add brown sugar and cream.
2. Stir, then add coconut and nuts. It will be thick.
3. Spread on top of baked cake and put under broiler just until brown. Watch carefully, as it can burn quickly.

Butter Tarts
Shana Gray

Preheat oven to 375

Pastry:
    1 pound lard
    Five cups flour
    1 tablespoon sugar
    One egg in measuring cup with 2 tablespoons vinegar, and measure to one cup with water

Directions
1. Combine all the ingredients, divided into three bottles. Can keep up to one week in the fridge or three weeks in the freezer.
2. Rollout and use round cutter for tart shape.
3. Place into muffin tins
4. Add a few drops of salt in the bottom of each tart cup.

Optional to add raisins or toasted pecans or walnuts to each cup

Butter Tart Filling
    ¼ cup butter softened
    ½ cup brown sugar
    ½ cup corn syrup – or can use maple syrup instead or equal of each to measure ½ cup
    One egg
    ¼ teaspoon salt

Directions

1. Cream all of the above ingredients together and fill to three quarters full each tart cup.
2. Cook for 20 minutes. The filling will become bubbly and rise up. Watch for pastry to become golden before removing. If filling spills over, while hot use a knife to score around the outside of the tart to separate filling from pan.

Polish Apple Cake
Shana Gray

Ingredients
2½ cups flour
⅔ cup sugar
2 tablespoons baking powder
1 teaspoon almond extract
1 tablespoon butter
6-8 apples peeled and chopped
6 ounces of oil
Two yolks and one whole egg
Cinnamon

Directions
1. Add half the sugar to the apples with the cinnamon and cook for 15 minutes. Cool.
2. Mix sugar, oil, eggs, almond and add to flour. Mix.
3. Divide dough, with one bigger
4. Grease and 9 x 9 pan and press the dough into the bottom and up the sides
5. Add apple mixture and drop the remaining pieces of dough on the top to cover
6. Big half an air to 45 minutes until dough is golden

Optional – sprinkle sugar on the top.

Polish Plum Cake
Shana Gray

Ingredients
½ cup butter
¾ cup white sugar
2 eggs
1 cup flour
1tbs baking powder
pinch salt
5-6 large plums halve and pitted (more if needed)
1 tsp cinnamon
icing sugar

Directions
1. Preheat oven to 350
2. Cream butter and sugar
3. Add eggs and beat well, stir in dry ingredients
4. Spoon batter into pan, arrange plums skin side up on the surface. If plums are big then quarter them
5. Sprinkle lightly with 1 tbs sugar and cinnamon
6. Bake 50 minutes or until don
7. Dust with icing sugar while warm

***

Shana Gray writes contemporary romance and women's fiction that just might make you laugh. With 30 books behind her, some translated into multiple languages, she's always eyeing the next story line. She lives in a small town in Ontario, Canada, is a mom of two grown sons, a brand new daughter-in-law, and is her black cat's human. When she's not writing or at her day job, she can be found daydreaming about life, usually with a glass of wine or cocktail in hand and making travel plans to far off lands to feed her wanderlust. Her newest series – Girl's Weekend Away – is out now.

Bread Pudding
Catherine Hope

My great grandmother's recipe and there are no measurements. It's by eye and taste.

Preheat oven to 350

Ingredients
Day old bread
Any kind of fruit – sultanas/mixed fruit
Butter
Vanilla and cinnamon
Flour – I put in a couple of tablespoons or until the bread is coated
Baking powder – I'd say a teaspoon
Salt
Sugar to taste

Directions
1. Soak bread in milk, not too wet and mix with hands until smooth
2. Add fruit and mix well
3. Add melted butter and vanilla, mix well
4. Add flour, baking powder, salt and mix well.
5. Add sugar to taste
6. Bake till cooked about 1¼ hours

Chapter Ten
Beverages

Margarita –
(2 people) or 1 writer who has had a really bad day.
Lisa Wells

Writing and drinking go together like love and romance. Maybe more so. It's not an easy career. Disappointment and nonconstructive criticism are hiding around every corner. But then, if you keep going, don't give up, make it to the next corner, and you'll often discover a wonderful review or a new book contract. Writing is the ultimate drinking game. Get a new book deal, have a drink. Get a one-star review, have two drinks. Make the NY Times top 100 have a pitcher of margaritas. The following are a couple of my go to drinks when my writing workday has gone both good and bad.

This is my go-to reward when I finish editing a book.

INGREDIENTS:
1 small can of frozen lime aid
1½ cans of water
Hand full of ice
2½ jiggers of Tequila
Drop of triple sec
Lime slice for garnishment

INSTRUCTIONS:
1. Mix in a pitcher and pour it over 2 salt rimmed cocktail glasses.

Bloody Mary – (1 person)
Lisa Wells

This is a great one to have while at a writer's retreat. It is a recipe that was given to me by a friend who knows how to party with the best of them.

INGREDIENTS:
4 ounces - Major Peters Original Bloody Mary Mix
Few splashes of Worcestershire sauce
2 ounces - Vodka
Caveners seasoned salt (3 to 4 shakes)
Valasic Pickle Juice (splash out of jar)
Pickle Spear
4-6 Ice Cubes

INSTRUCTIONS:
1. Place the ice cubes in a tall glass.
2. Measure in all the ingredients.
3. Using a long spoon, stir until the ice is coated in the ingredients.
4. Garnish with a toothpick loaded with green olives and lay on top.
5. Add celery stick (or spicy green beans, jalapeno pepper, etc.) and enjoy. Don't forget to add the pickle.

Hot Spice Wine (for a crowd)
Lisa Wells

Great for a gathering of writers in the winter

INGREDIENTS:
½ package of red hots
1 can of pineapple juice
5 cinnamon sticks stuck in middle of slices of fruit (like an orange)
Whole cloves stuck in fruit (in each slice of fruit stick several cloves)
JUG OF GALLO ROSE WINE

INSTRUCTIONS:
1. Combine (ALL BUT THE WINE) and melt (in crockpot)
2. Simmer
3. After all is ready, add a jug of Gallo Rose Wine.

***

Lisa Wells writes romantic comedy with enough steam to fog your eyeglasses, your brain, and sometimes your Kindle screen. On the other hand, her eighty-year-old mother-in-law has read Lisa's steamiest book and lived to offer her commentary. Which went something like this: *You used words I've never heard of…*

She lives in Missouri with her husband and slightly-chunky rescue dog. Lisa loves dark chocolate, red wine, and those rare mornings when her skinny jeans fit. Which isn't often, considering the first two entries on her love-it list.

Summer Evening White Sangria
Catherine Stuart

This recipe comes from my dad. He's originally from Switzerland, so he's always introducing me to new ingredients, including kirsch—a not terribly sweet fruit brandy, typically made from cherries, but also from pears. It can go into a seafood bisque or a cheese fondue. Or white sangria.

I make it in the summer, when anything else would be too heavy in the heat. It's best enjoyed while sitting on the porch, in the early evening. Also recommended: multiple fans blowing, lots of bug spray, music playing in the background, and family or friends—preferably the ones who know all the best gossip.

Ingredients
      1 bottle of light white wine, such as pinot bianco
      ⅓ cup of pear kirsch, brandy, or white rum
      1 orange
      1 peach or nectarine
      1 plum
      Sprite, 7Up, or other carbonated beverage

Step 1. Prep the fruit.
1. Chop up the peach and the plum into small, bite-size pieces.
2. Cut ½ of the orange into slices. Set aside the other ½ of the orange.
3. Feel free to add any additional fruit that strikes your fancy, such as apples, pears, or cherries.

Step 2. Soak the fruit in the brandy.

1. Allow the chopped fruit to soak in the brandy for at least an hour, stirring occasionally.

Step 3. Mix the drink.

2. Juice the remaining ½ of the orange into a large pitcher.
3. Add the brandy, brandy-soaked fruit, and wine into the pitcher.
4. Top with Sprite and lightly stir.

Note: Adjust the amount of Sprite and brandy to how strong you would like your sangria.

Chapter Eleven
Extra Goodies

Steak Marinade
Brenda Margriet

We love to cook over an open fire, and steak is a must-have when we are camping.

Ingredients
2 tablespoons Montreal Steak Spice Rub (the paste, not the dry spice)
1 tablespoon soya sauce
1 tablespoon olive oil
1 tablespoon red wine (optional, but good)
2 steaks (your cut of choice)

Directions
1. Spoon half the marinade into a freezer bag. Place steaks in bag, spoon remaining marinade over top. Seal bag and make sure marinade has coated the steaks.
2. Marinate 1 to 2 hours at room temperature or up to 24 hours refrigerated.

*Kitchen Hack: Freeze steaks right in the bag once coated in marinade. Let thaw prior to use to marinate further.

Riley's BBQ Sauce
Gail Chianese

My grandfather was pretty helpless in the kitchen unless he was making soup or standing over a barbeque. As far back as I can remember, he made his own sauce, slathered it over chicken or ribs, and threw it on a big brick grill in the backyard. This stuff was indeed "finger-licking good." One of his friends even submitted it to Sunset Magazine, who published the recipe.

It wasn't the 4th of July if we didn't have Grandpa's BBQ sauce.

Ingredients
1 bottle ketchup
1 bottle chili sauce
1 c. oil
½ c. vinegar or wine
½ c. water
1 large onion minced (can use any kind, I prefer sweet)
1 clove garlic, minced
Dash of Worcestershire sauce
Dash of Tabasco

Directions
1. Bring all ingredients to a boil and simmer, at least one hour or longer if possible.
2. Slather over your favorite protein and grill. Freezes well.

***

Gail Chianese is a multi-published author of contemporary romance, romantic mystery, and women's fiction. Originally from California, (she's lived in eight states and three countries thanks to the US Navy) and now calls Connecticut home with her real-life hero of a husband, her three amazing kids and too many animals to count.

'GOING GREENS' SMOOTHIE
Sarah Andre

In 2017 I was a finalist for the most prestigious romance writing award (the RWA Rita®) and had only a few months to lose a lot of weight for the national ceremony. I cashed in my savings and indulged in personal chef services to get the smartest, most efficient weight loss in the shortest amount of time. This is one of her recipes, so you'll get to taste what a fun and nutritious few months I had working to fit into my dream dress.

P.S. The romantic suspense novel that finaled was *Tall, Dark and Damaged.*

Ingredients
   1 sliced cucumber
   1 Granny Smith apple
   1 C spinach leaves
   1 small orange
   1 small piece of fresh ginger, chopped
   1 medium sized banana
   ½ C water
   ½ C almond milk

Combine ingredients in a blender until smooth and creamy. Green goodness never tasted so good!

Serves 2

Quarantine Balls
(a/k/a Healthy Granola Treats)
Beth Carter

I named these healthy snacks quarantine balls during the pandemic for obvious reasons. I almost can't wait until my bananas ripen so I can make them!

Ingredients
½ cup peanut butter, heaping (low-fat is fine)
2 ripe bananas, smashed
2 cups oats, uncooked

*Optional ingredients: ¼ cup pecans, chopped and ½ tsp. cinnamon. (I prefer the classic, three-ingredient recipe.)

Directions
1. Preheat oven to 350 degrees.
2. Combine peanut butter and oats. Will be a thick consistency.
3. Add bananas and fold until moistened.
4. Roll into balls.
5. Bake on an ungreased cookie sheet for 15 minutes.

NOTE: May substitute almond butter or cashew butter for the peanut butter.

Yield: 24 treats

Aunt Lee's Hot Fudge
Tracy Brogan

This is a favorite family recipe, and "Aunt Lee" is actually my mom. My sister likes to make a big batch of this in December and then give it away as Christmas gifts and we are not above stealing it from each other. It's delicious on ice cream but it's also pretty darn good straight from the refrigerator on a spoon. My mom passed away at sixty-six when I was just twenty-six so making this recipe makes me feel very nostalgic.

Ingredients
¾ cup chocolate chips
½ cup butter
1 tsp vanilla
1 can (12 oz.) evaporated milk
2 cups powdered sugar

Directions
1. Slowly melt the butter and chocolate chips over low heat.
2. When smooth, add vanilla and evaporated milk.
3. When that's thoroughly blended, fold in powdered sugar and keep stirring.
4. Bring to a medium boil and keep stirring for 8 minutes.
5. Serve over ice cream.

Hot fudge can be stored in the refrigerator and reheated.

Peanut Butter Dog Pill Balls
Tracey Devlyn

Earlier this year, my sweet red Doberman got really sick. I had to figure out how to get my boy to take a half dozen pills (mornings and evenings) when he had no interest in food and could barely walk. Finding this recipe saved us both so much stress.

Makes approx. 120 pill balls

Ingredients
>1 cup peanut butter (MUST BE all natural peanut butter; NO Xylitol)
>1.5 cups tapioca flour
>1 tablespoon molasses
>½ cup milk, plus 2 tablespoons

Directions
1. In a medium bowl, add peanut butter and molasses; mix well.
2. Add ½ cup milk; mix well.
3. Add ½ cup of flour; mix well. Repeat two more times until all the flour is incorporated.
4. Now set aside your mixing spoon and use your hand to knead the dough until it becomes one big ball. If the dough is too crumbly, add a tablespoon (or two) of milk. Does it feel too wet? Add a little more flour. You're looking for a consistency that will allow you to easily

push a pill into the ball. If it's too dry, the ball will crumble. If it's too wet, the balls will stick together in a gooey mess at the bottom of the storage container/bag.

5. Pinch off dough to create ½ inch balls; squeeze the dough with your fingers a few times before rolling it between your palms to form the balls.
6. Place finished balls in a plastic bag or other air tight container.
7. Refrigerate to keep pill balls fresh.

Liver Cookies for Dogs
Kelly Garcia

I made liver cookies for the first time when I got my first dog. I used them as training treats. The kitchen smelled like liver, but it's worth it to see how happy the treats made my dog.

Ingredients
1½ to 2 cups flour (all-purpose, whole wheat, or oat)
1 cup liver (beef or chicken)
¼ cup applesauce
water

Directions
1. Place liver in food processor or blender and blend until smooth.
2. Add applesauce and then enough flour to form a sticky cookie dough texture. If needed add a small amount of water.
3. Bake at 350°F for 20 minutes.
4. Cut into small pieces.
5. Give to dogs sparingly as a treat.

Index

A.S. Fenichel, 107, 109, 112, 231, 232

Aliza Mann, 11, 12, 117, 118, 193

Belle Calhoune, 135, 136, 251

Beth Carter, 43, 125, 282, 307

Betty Bolté, 113, 114, 149, 150

Beverly Jenkins, 237

Blake Oliver, 105, 106, 200

Brenda Margriet, 189, 190, 303

Casey Hagen, 17, 18, 255

Catherine Hope, 141, 142, 291

Catherine Stuart, 19, 20, 123, 124, 298

Cathryn Marr, 225, 226

Cathy McDavid, 5, 7, 23, 163, 164

Collette Cameron, 181, 201

Deb Kastner, 8, 144

Dee Davis, 35, 45, 245

Ella Quinn, 31, 133

Gail Chianese, 29, 30, 131, 304, 305

Gemma Brocato, 13, 14, 72, 73, 265

Heather Heyford, 15, 16, 165, 166

Jennifer Bray-Weber, 139, 140, 273

Jo McNally, 89, 90, 219, 285

JoAnn Brown, 69, 70, 247, 248

Jodi Thomas, 211, 212

JoMarie DeGioia, 207, 208

Judi Fennell, 129, 130, 242, 243, 244

K.D. Garcia, 41, 75

Kat Martin, 137, 138

Kelly Garcia, 311

Kristan Higgins, 3, 4, 199

Leslie Hachtel, 87, 126, 221, 223, 224, 277

Leslie Scott, 151, 153

Linda Warren, 169, 170, 171, 253

Lisa Kessler, 195, 278

Lisa Wells, 295, 296, 297

Lori Ryan, 97, 98

Lori Wilde, 79, 81, 82

Lorraine Heath, 239, 240, 241

Lucy Farago, 92, 94, 259, 261

Mary Jo Putney, 145, 146, 167

Mary K. Tilghman, 91

Melanie Greene, 122, 187, 188

Meredith Bond, 77, 78, 157, 158

Mindy Neff, 25, 27, 154, 183, 262

Nancy C. Weeks, 175, 176, 279, 281

Nikki Brock, 63, 64, 132, 257, 258

Nikki Sloane, 99, 100, 263

Nina Crespo, 101, 103, 104, 229, 230

Nisha Sharma, 47, 48, 269, 270

Penelope Janu, 159, 160, 233, 246

Piper G. Huguley, 33, 34, 217, 218

RaeAnne Thayne, 9, 10, 115, 116

Roni Denholtz, 143

Sarah Andre, 42, 49, 88, 209, 210, 306

Shana Gray, 287, 289, 290

Sharon Sala, 65, 67, 68

Sheila Roberts, 36, 37, 203, 204

Shirley Jump, 213, 215, 216

Stacy Finz, 50, 52, 53, 61, 62

Stephanie J. Scott, 191, 192, 271, 272

Susan Wiggs, 147, 148, 283

Susan Wisnewski, 46, 268

Teri Wilson, 28, 121, 185

Terri Osburn, 119, 120, 227, 228

Terri Reed, 95, 96

Toni Anderson, 83, 84, 177, 178

Tracey Devlyn, 85, 86, 275, 309

Tracey Livesay, 59, 60, 249

Tracy Brogan, 173, 174, 184, 205, 308

Valerie Clarizio, 71, 155, 267

Thank you for buying our
cookbook to support ProLiteracy.

We wish you Bon Appetit
and, of course,
Happily Ever Afters.